Account Management

Ken Langdon

SALES

12.05

- Fast-track route to understanding key account management and its importance to a successful and profitable business

- Covers increasing the volume, profitability and predictability of key account sales, a team-based approach to account selling, planning for long-term account management and allocation of resources

- Examples and lessons using SWOT analysis on the mission statements of a number of companies from different sectors

- Includes a resource section and access to a free website for insights, ideas and the best practice in account management, as well as ten key steps to practicing successful account management, key concepts and thinkers and an FAQ section

>>EXPRESS EXEC.COM<<
essential management thinking at your fingertips

First Published 2003 by
Capstone Publishing Limited (a Wiley company)
8 Newtec Place
Magdalen Road
Oxford OX4 1RE
United Kingdom
http://www.capstoneideas.com

CIP catalogue records for this book are available from the British Library and the US Library of Congress

ISBN 13: 978-1-84112-458-2

Wiley also publishes its books in a variety of electronic formats. Some content that appears in print may not be available in electronic books.

Websites often change their contents and addresses; details of sites listed in this book were accurate at the time of writing, but may change.

Substantial discounts on bulk quantities of Capstone Books are available to corporations, professional associations and other organizations. For details telephone Capstone Publishing on (+44-1865-798623), fax (+44-1865-240941) or email (info@wiley-capstone.co.uk).

FSC

Mixed Sources
Product group from well-managed forests and other controlled sources

Cert no. SGS-COC-2953
www.fsc.org
© 1996 Forest Stewardship Council

Contents

Introduction to ExpressExec

ExpressExec is a completely up-to-date resource of current business practice, accessible in a number of ways – anytime, anyplace, anywhere. ExpressExec combines best practice cases, key ideas, action points, glossaries, further reading, and resources.

Each module contains 10 individual titles that cover all the key aspects of global business practice. Written by leading experts in their field, the knowledge imparted provides executives with the tools and skills to increase their personal and business effectiveness, benefiting both employee and employer.

ExpressExec is available in a number of formats:

» **Print** – 120 titles available through retailers or printed on demand using any combination of the 1200 chapters available.
» **E-Books** – e-books can be individually downloaded from Express-Exec.com or online retailers onto PCs, handheld computers, and e-readers.
» **Online** – http://www.expressexec.wiley.com/ provides fully searchable access to the complete ExpressExec resource via the Internet – a cost-effective online tool to increase business expertise across a whole organization.

» **ExpressExec Performance Support Solution (EEPSS)** – a software solution that integrates ExpressExec content with interactive tools to provide organizations with a complete internal management development solution.
» **ExpressExec Rights and Syndication** – ExpressExec content can be licensed for translation or display within intranets or on Internet sites.

To find out more visit www.ExpressExec.com or contact elound@wiley-capstone.co.uk.

Introduction to Account Management

This chapter considers how key accounts arise and gives a précis of how to handle them:

» in a partnership of open cooperation; and
» using specific processes to encourage the relationship and thus increase the volume, profitability, and predictability of sales.

Whether you like it or not, some accounts are key. Whether you are selling complex products or services involving high technology, or selling fast-moving consumer goods in complex marketplaces facing change and competition, you will have some key accounts. When a new company starts with a new product, the product is the focus of the selling effort and the key element of the first sales campaigns. Success is very much tied up in whether you have invented the better mousetrap or not.

In technology terms the product will first of all strike interest in the minds of technologists. They will examine it and decide if it has a place in the way that they do things currently. The seller of the product is often its inventor. Inventors have an extraordinary ability to handle technical doubts and fears about their invention. After all it is not until they have thought all of these through themselves that they announce the product to the world.

It is probably up to the customer to find the applications to begin with, but the moment the first sale is made the situation changes. The first customer is immediately key to the success of the product and the company selling it.

The introduction of a new product in the fast-moving consumer goods marketplace gives rise to a similar situation. This time the key account probably chooses itself by the similarity of how the two companies see the marketplace. It is also a function of volume. The key account is the one that will use up the production capacity the selling company plans to utilize.

As time passes, key accounts in all circumstances need special management. How we measure customer satisfaction, how we set our prices and discounts, and whom we speak to in the account itself tends to be different in the small percentage of the market which is of significant importance to the selling company.

You cannot calculate it mathematically, but it is something like the 80–20 rule – 80% of our most important business is done with 20% of our customers. Or potentially this will be the case.

KEY ACCOUNTS NEED DIFFERENT PROCESSES

It has long been the case in high technology that the tightness of the relationship between key accounts and the selling company has dictated that the selling company approaches these top accounts differently.

You can sum it up in a number of ways. The two companies know much more about each other. There is openness in the relationship reflecting the fact that both companies gain from allowing the other to get very close to its plans and strategies. As long as the selling company is adding value beyond the simple delivery of product, the customer will agree to sharing information and even plans with its supplier.

In fast-moving consumer goods, account management is proving more and more to hold the key to protecting and improving market share, while at the same time maintaining profitability.

Alliances are formed and last for very lengthy periods of time. The relationship is close and mutually dependent. But we must not go too far. In the end the account sales team and the customer work for different companies. Their fundamental objectives and strategies may have lots in common, but there is never any doubt where their priorities lie.

We must expect openness and confidences in a working partnership, but we must not expect a customer with whom we are continuously negotiating business deals to reveal absolutely all. No more than we, the selling team, will to the customer.

What we need are processes that support the partnership in the long term, provide the customer with the business benefits of excellent products and services, and the selling company with a profitable and predictable stream of sales.

Definition of Terms: What is Account Management?

This chapter covers the definition of the following terms:

» solution selling, account management, and the objectives of account management and solution selling;
» producing plans to manage an account for profit;
» salespeople as hunters and farmers; and
» teams, virtual teams, and working partnerships.

SOLUTION SELLING

The difference in the approach to major sales campaigns in key accounts is mainly found in the involvement of the selling team with the customer's business. The team needs to understand the impact of the products under consideration on the actual financial results and image of the customer.

In high technology, for example, such a sales campaign would be an opportunity, probably in competition, to supply products and services that will enable the customer to do things differently. It may be a multi-million pound deal, or it may be a small project of great strategic importance to the customer. In either case, the selling company needs to understand enough about the customer's business to be able to couch the proposal in their terms and identify and agree the financial and other benefits of the project.

In fast-moving consumer goods (FMCG) the example may be to do with a particular promotion to which the selling company wishes the customer to apply resources of people and money. It may be using combinations of marketing information to extend markets and market share.

This type of business-oriented selling we will call "solution selling" as opposed to "product-based selling."

To engage in solution selling we need to examine two key questions.

1 How do account managers gather the information they need to produce an effective solution-selling campaign?
2 How does the selling team martial its resources to establish a persuasive business argument for the sale and sell it to the customer?

This topic is covered in the ExpressExec title *Complex Sales*, by the same author and using similar types of consistent processes.

ACCOUNT MANAGEMENT

Moving towards solution selling is the first mark distinguishing the key account from any other account. However, the real rewards from professional account management go beyond mere customer-oriented sales campaigns. Professional account management involves the creation and nurturing of a working partnership with a long-term perspective. This raises big questions of investment in key accounts. Companies expect higher profitability and loyalty from key accounts. They also expect reference sites for future customers and early sales of new products. There are a number of processes required to achieve all of that. These processes and concepts are at once straightforward to define and quite difficult to put in place practically.

Account managers need to establish their objectives in considering their key account approach, and they need to get many people in their own organization to buy into the practicality of the new processes. And they need time. Long-term plans take a while to gain momentum, and some companies are put off by the wait. But the power of the joint plan between the supplier and customer will produce such benefits in terms of revenue and profit that the supplier must bite the bullet and give the team a chance to make it happen.

THE PLAN'S THE THING

In the end, an agreed approach to all aspects of customer care and selling emerges as the result of a plan. This is a practical guide to account management. It seeks to put the reality into phrases such as "building a business partnership" – a concept claimed by many companies but achieved by few. I will try to explain in usable terms what goes into an account plan and the other forms and processes of account management. But be warned, if such processes are badly presented to the salespeople, they will groan and complain that the bureaucracy of their masters is stifling their sales talent and leaving no time to get on with the selling.

This is a major paradox. We expect a key account to yield higher results than a normal territory. Yet we have to expend money and energy on matters not directly aimed at taking more orders and doing more business. Put another way, account management is where the argument between operating for the short term and striving to meet strategic objectives hits the front-line troops.

You need a balance. If you are to get competitive advantage by dealing more comprehensively with key accounts, you have to have a long-term plan. At the same time you have to satisfy the needs of first-line sales managers whose bonus scheme and, indeed, whose essence is about achieving today's sales results and this year's target.

MANAGING ACCOUNTS FOR PROFIT

A New York salesperson of printer/scanner/fax machines had his territory or patch defined as the Empire State Building. The territory was just the right size to ensure that he could get round all the prospects and serve his customers in a year. He put a machine under his arm, started at the top of the building in January, and sold his way down to the ground floor by the following Christmas. Good cost-effective selling with the minimum of traveling time.

The question arises: does the salesperson look after the territory differently if, instead of having a thousand individual customers, they had all belonged to the same corporation? Table 2.1 outlines some of

Table 2.1

All separate companies	A single corporation
The salesperson can get to the decision makers in each of the separate businesses. He or she is never far from the source of money and purchasing power	Even if head office has delegated peripheral buying to the subsidiary companies and divisions, it can always undo that and draw back spending power to the center
The buyers in the individual offices make the technical decision, either the purchasing manager or the technical department if such a body exists	It is often the case that head office decides technological strategy and imposes it on the divisions of the business. The situation is at its most difficult if the salesperson is working on a division on floor 3, while his or her competitor is working on the head office technical managers on floor 34
The line managers, the people responsible for making the revenues and profits of the business, are all accessible in a small discrete organization. They are financial, technical, and user buyers (terms we will examine in the course of this book) all rolled into one	If one corporation owns the whole block, then access to line management can be more difficult. The fast-moving consumer goods salesperson risks being confined to the buying department, or the computer salesperson to the technical department

Table 2.1 (*continued*)

All separate companies	A single corporation
If the salesperson believes it to be a good thing to offer an incentive to one company, no other business will know about it or ask for the same treatment	If the salesperson gives a concession to one division of an organization, then other divisions will use that number as the starting point of the next negotiation
If something goes wrong with one of the machines the salesperson has sold the grief is isolated. Whether it is the supplier's fault (for example, a Friday afternoon piece of hardware) or the customer's fault (for example, poor training causing finger trouble) it will only affect the individual company	Bad news spreads like wildfire. The story of dissatisfaction will go round the corporation – causing at best delays in getting further orders while the problem is fixed, or at worst a review of the buying policy and the possible removal of the supplier from the permitted list
If someone in the smaller business buys something for no great reason, or a more expensive model than required because they like the look of it, that will be the end of the matter	There are always auditors – financial and business process auditors. They will demand to know the return on investment of the product being bought and want blow-by-blow reasons for choosing anything except the cheapest option
Competitive pressures are present but limited in scope. If a competitor is doing well in one company the salesperson can afford to ignore the whole company. Just drop down a floor and start again	Salespeople in this environment cannot ignore competitors wherever they are. Any subsidiary or division that is going down a particular buying route can eventually have an impact on other divisions or even on the whole corporation

the key issues making the situation totally different in the case of the large organization or key account.

This ''arbitrage'' effect becomes even more severe when we look at the more realistic case: that the large corporation is not just in the Empire State Building, but all over the world.

An American computer manufacturer had a very profitable subsidiary in the UK. The subsidiary imported product from the USA and sold it at the prevailing market price in the UK. For various reasons, to do with the price of petrol amongst others, there was a significant move in the dollar/sterling exchange rate. At first the UK company was unaffected by the change, since the parent company set the transfer price which it charged the subsidiary on a quarterly basis. Then it was delighted by the change as the market price in the UK had not changed and they were buying cheaper from their own manufacturing department's internal charge.

Then it went nastily wrong. One of their global accounts discovered that it could buy the products cheaper in its USA company and import them to the UK themselves. This cut out the UK subsidiary completely. Not only that, but the global corporation realized that if it could do the deal for companies internal to the corporation why not for others? It started up a business bringing in computers from the USA and selling at a considerable discount to the UK price. From its position of comfort the UK subsidiary was now competing with its own products at a price disadvantage. The difference between these two scenarios is what we will call account management.

THE OBJECTIVES OF ACCOUNT MANAGEMENT

Even at this early stage it is worth taking a moment to ensure that we recognize why sales teams concentrate their efforts on key accounts. In a nutshell, here are the objectives of account management:

» to gain market share;
» to improve profitability;
» to produce reference sites which will assist with other sales camp-aigns;
» to keep your product developers and marketing people up to date with what the market is looking for now and in the future;
» to improve the productivity of the sales and support resources; and
» to get more predictable sales which are forecast in advance.

SELLING THE CUSTOMER A SOLUTION

The Empire State Building is of such a size that it is going to be difficult for the salesperson to understand the business benefits his or her machines are giving to all the customers. They do not buy one if they do not need one. Beyond that it is not the job of the product seller to help the customer understand the differences which using the machine is going to have on the bottom line of the business.

Solution selling to key accounts is different. The salesperson is working on the premise that a customer who understands what a product or service is actually achieving for the business is the sort of customer who buys more of that product or service. The aim of solution selling becomes not just to make profits for the selling company, but also to make profits for the buyer.

An account manager who was selling computer systems to a major telephone company struggled with this concept. He found it "intellectually dishonest" to take an objective that had to do with the health of the buying company as opposed to the profits of the selling company. The customer called a halt at one point, did an audit of all computer systems and discovered that he had more than enough and that some were simply not paying their way. That same account manager was then on the defensive, trying to justify after the event purchases the customer had made.

The objectives of solution selling are:

» to make more sales by working with the customer to understand the return on investment offered by your products and services;
» to produce satisfied customers;
» to gain competitive edge by recognizing earlier than your competitors where the customer should invest next; and
» to build customer loyalty by giving no reasons for them to look elsewhere.

The role of account management in promoting solution selling is to break down the natural customer barriers to suppliers getting as close to the heart of their organization as good solution selling implies.

HUNTERS AND FARMERS

It is useful to divide the selling job into "hunting" or "farming." Hunting is about bringing in new customers, while farming is about increasing the amount and type of business you do with your existing customers. The skills are different and an important aspect of people selection is to consider how much of each activity the job involves.

For hunters the main requirement is persistence and the ability to take knocks. Theirs is the job that has them trying to get interviews with strangers who may not only be unaware of their needs but antagonistic to an unsolicited approach, whether on the telephone or in person. Hunters generally work quickly, have short attention spans and feel very dissatisfied if complications of product or decision-making processes intrude on their getting to the point of closing a sale. They are opportunists and in most cases need watching to make sure that the product being sold is suitable and will work as promised by the salesperson.

Some would say that it is the hunters who give salespeople a bad name. There is some truth in that, but they are also the people who make innovation possible and *en masse* bear a lot of responsibility for driving the dollar round in a growth economy. The hunter is the salesperson who gets a high level of job satisfaction in getting a first order from a new customer. A seller of reprographics expressed it as follows:

> "You actually have to start by getting yourself invited into the buyer's office. Then you must convince a probable skeptic that what you are offering has benefits over continuing with the people he or she has previously done business with.
>
> "Then you have to find a project, bid for it, and win it. The great feeling is that you made it happen, unless you had made the first move and then followed through, that company would have remained loyal to its existing suppliers."

This is the typical conversation of a hunter. You will recognize some other phrases and sayings in their coffee-break chat – "I thought I'd do one more door," "Stitched him up in no time flat."

Every salesperson has to have some of the hunter attributes. A good farmer who hates or claims to be bad at new business selling may be too slow to go for the order or not sufficiently assertive to win against the competition. Once again we see the balance that is crucial for a professional account manager – between hustling to get things done and farming for the long term.

Farmers develop skills in long-term relationship building and deep knowledge of a customer's business. A professional sales team selling machine tools, for example, will build over the years a database of customer knowledge the customer itself may envy. The benefits to management of professional farmers comes in terms of predictable orders, competitive intelligence, market changes, and much more.

In FMCG (fast-moving consumer goods) this knowledge is equally important. The account manager needs to know the detail of the customer's strategy and interface to the consumer. He or she then needs to know the results of market research and, of course, of actual sales. The more he or she knows about how the customers sell the product, the more able he or she is to make innovative proposals and achieve stretching sales targets.

An aiming point of professional account management is to be able to hold a joint planning session. The sales team works with the customer to build a plan for the next year in detail, and three years in outline.

When this happens it is a sure sign that your company has truly created the "working partnership" and "added value." A lot of salespeople talk about these concepts but misunderstand the difficulties and timescales involved in setting the partnership up and adding real value.

TEAMS AND VIRTUAL TEAMS

A key attribute of the good account manager is the ability to use only charismatic power to motivate people to achieve their part in his or her plan.

Best practice has the account manager responsible only for the performance of the company in an account. He or she is not responsible for the "pay and rations" of the salespeople and support people involved in the account.

The account manager for an advertising agency who looks after the Proctor and Gamble account worldwide might have over 100 people working in sales, support, and creative roles. They all probably work for different line managers. This gives an idea of the complexity of implementing a plan without having direct control over the necessary resources.

Add that the account is live on 5 continents and 150 countries and the problem looks formidable. It is formidable, and the supervision and motivation of "virtual teams" needs attention not only in terms of business processes, but also in terms of the skill involved in the management of people by leadership and motivation.

So far we have looked at the implementation teams working on the products and services being supplied. We need to take into account the senior management teams in both companies. Frequently the situation arises where a high achiever account manager has become a senior manager in the supplying firm.

This poses new problems. The customer's people will probably want to continue to deal with the person they know despite the fact they have moved into other roles. Account managers need diplomacy as well as business processes to deal with a situation involving egos as well as business logic.

WORKING PARTNERSHIPS

It is not possible to give a convincing definition of a working partnership until we have discussed all the aspects of business and account planning which come within the remit of a professional account manager.

The key to it, however, is the concept of joint planning. For the moment, therefore, we will use the incomplete definition of a working partnership as:

» a working partnership exists when the selling company is involved in the customer's planning processes, and when the customer is involved in the supplier's planning processes.

KEY LEARNING POINTS

Account management is a combination of selling solutions to customer problems to give this year's sales and profit streams, and putting in place and maintaining a strategy for working with the customer in a relationship that makes the next years of sales predictable and profitable.

The Evolution of Account Management

This chapter looks at the evolution, through trial and error over the years, of current thinking about account management in terms of:

» the military origins of strategy and team planning;
» the organization of the account sales and support force; and
» best practice in the timing of account planning and review through a company year.

A POSSIBLE STARTING POINT

The evolution of many management processes starts from the military. In earlier times, indeed, the definition of "strategy" was "the art of planning and directing large military movements and the operations of war." An account manager needs a strategy to map the future, setting out, amongst other things, what products they are going to sell, to which parts of the customer, and when. So, as in a military setting, a strategy is a declaration of intent, defining where you want to be in the long term.

Now, when non-military people think about a military strategy, they think about a theater of war, where a significant difference between military command and management is that lower ranks have no right whatsoever to question, or to fail to act on, an instruction. However, the logistics of getting people and materials to the right place in a military situation require the cooperation of team members and their contribution to the creativity of a plan in just the same way as in an organizational team. So the second evolution of current thinking about account planning – team planning – also probably had its origins in the military.

NCR AND IBM

The modern concept of account management can be traced back in the first place to NCR in America, who are credited with forming the first sales training department and to the NCR protégée Tom Watson, who took the idea forward when he left NCR (or was thrown out, according to what you believe) and founded IBM. Certainly, the requirement for a decent strategy and account plan was crucial when selling the large mainframe computers of the sixties to eighties. They required a merging of the customer's long-term business plan, the need for application solutions to give real business benefits, and the two technology strategies – customer's and supplier's.

Many training consultancies and process consultants have taken this work forward. The work of Kepner Tregoe, for example, contributed towards the current concept of team planning, and it is the evolution of this process that forms the building blocks of a sales plan and a campaign plan.

ORGANIZATION AND STRUCTURE

It is true to say that in the evolution of account management someone has tried everything. It is not possible to generalize about how a company should organize its account management effort. From experience we can make a number of suggestions which at least raise the issues you need to resolve. Most process consultants would agree, however, with the following now tried and tested route.

It is most important to bear in mind that management has to find a balance between lack of stability in their organization and an overly rigid adherence to the current structure. Just as in any form of general management, the winners are the ones who recognize the need for change before they are forced into it by a collapse of revenue or profit for whatever reason. Who, at the time of its predominance, would have thought that the great IBM would, for a period of time, actually become an old-fashioned basket case? Taking such a possibility into consideration has to be part of an account manager's philosophy. Nothing is permanent.

IF YOU HAVE TO CHANGE MARKETS, DO IT IN TIME

Two independent consultants, previously colleagues in a larger company, had made a decent living out of working in the computer industry for a variety of clients. In the late eighties they were discussing the problems of the established computer majors and swapping stories about the statements of senior people in the computer world they had spoken to recently. In piecing it all together, an alarming picture arose. It became clear that everyone was predicting disaster for everyone except themselves. No one escaped. If company A said that company B was failing to adapt to the new situation, then you could be sure that company C was saying the same of company A. And so on.

The consultants mused about whether the prognostications were true or not. (In the great majority of cases they were true.) The two colleagues decided it would be imprudent to do nothing in the face of such evidence. They gave each other the target of getting at least one new client each in a different industry. They chose the telecommunications sector, which was in a phase of rapid growth. Scared of losing face by failing to keep their side of the bargain, the consultants put together sales campaigns and duly delivered one new client each. Two years later, their businesses were dominated by telecommunications, which was producing more than 80% of their revenues. Meanwhile, the computer industry had gone into total disarray, and the consultancy field was flooded with hundreds of new independents who had been released from the computer industry under the newly coined euphemism "downsizing."

This lack of permanence is true of any account management organization. What works now may not do so well when the company has more accounts, or the market changes.

Against this requirement for flexibility is the opposing need for allowing a structure time to prove itself. Digging up the carrots to see how the roots are doing can upset and demotivate account teams. Continuous change makes the teams wonder if the senior management is in control or has a strategy at all. I will take the issues for deliberation as follows:

» profit center management
» reporting structures
» number of accounts in a territory.

Profit center management

I think the case is now proved that a salesperson makes a poor profit center. If you give a salesperson the automatic right, for example, to offer a 10% discount, he or she will tend to make the concession too early in the sales process. In fact, salespeople have a tendency to give their best shot on price the moment the customer suggests they may have a price disadvantage. In my opinion, a salesperson should be encouraged to seek volume, to sell as high a value of product as possible at the price on the price list. If they know what the transfer prices are they will berate management for concessions down to a price which is easier for them to sell at. On a need to know basis, then, the salesperson can operate quite happily with a hazy idea of the margins and costs of selling which management are working with.

In account management the situation can be very different. Particularly in the case of a key account manager who has other salespeople taking the orders in the account, it may be advisable to organize the account as a profit center. At least account managers' profit and loss accounts should show the transfer price or gross margin as well as the costs of the resources deployed on the account. If it is a worldwide account this can be difficult to organize from a management information point of view. But it is not good enough to put this up as an excuse if the profit and loss account is the right way to go.

A profit center is truly a profit center when the manager is given the responsibility of the asset base he or she is using to make money. I have seen only failed attempts to put asset management down to first line management. If you ask account managers to look after the company's assets it tends to take their eye off the customer orientation.

FINANCE PRESSURE CAN BECOME COUNTER PRODUCTIVE

I worked with a company which, because it had got itself into serious financial problems, recruited a new managing director whose background was finance. He rightly diagnosed the root of the problem as being in sales management. The sales managers were used to working with high gross margins and had developed expensive habits of discounting and providing free support. They were not "spending the company's money as though it were their own" and the company had become vulnerable to any slow down of revenue which threatened to cause further cash problems.

By Herculean effort the company's accountants produced the information and systems to push real profit center management down to first line sales managers. This lasted only for one year. The sales managers became totally introverted about their p and l's and balance sheets. If, for example, a salesperson wanted to offer a trade-in of an old product to support a campaign to sell a new one, sales managers would make a huge effort to unload the second-hand product on someone else's territory. If they failed to do so, the product was charged to their profit and loss account. They would disallow sales in favor of making money in some other way.

It cannot be said that the year-long experiment did not work. Once the situation was made more standard by lifting the level of profit centers, the first line managers were much more conscious of selling profitably.

Reporting structures – the account team

I believe that salespeople should report to sales managers. This means that where a key account manager has sub-accountees selling for him or her in different locations, possibly all over the world, there is only charismatic power and leadership available to the account manager. This will only work if the planning regime is tight, and sales managers have agreed in writing the amount of time their salespeople will work on the various accounts.

There is a supply and demand situation here. If it is easier to achieve a sales target with customers who are not in a particular key account, then that is what salespeople will do. It is up to the account manager to produce an account environment which enables the sub-accountees to sell more easily to their customers.

The same is true for support and maintenance management. However, where there is a considerable amount of, for example, technical support involved in every sale, then there is an important decision to be made. At what level do the sales and support organizations come under the same manager? It is almost certain that it should be well below the managing director.

The most successful organizations I have seen have had support managers reporting into sales at second or even first line management. You need an audit function, of course, with senior support people in staff jobs with a remit to ensure the integrity of what the support people under sales management are doing.

Number of accounts in a territory

If you are looking after companies which are in the top 500 in size, then you have to be practical about your workload. If you consider the amount of effort required to carry out all the professional processes in this book and then keep the plans up to date, you can see that in all probability only one can receive this full treatment.

If you only have one account then there is no problem. Carry out the processes on the parts of the customer where there is current or potential return. If you have more than one account, you need to pick one out for the full treatment and then look for practical shortcuts for the others. In the next part of this chapter I will make a suggestion as to what these shortcuts may be.

CREATING A PLAN

Not much evolution is involved to identify the steps in a creative planning process. The first steps are:

» analyze the current situation (commonly called "environmental analysis");
» set the objectives that the team decides are the most stretching which can be achieved given the current position; and
» agree the actions required to achieve those objectives.

Fig. 3.1 shows the general planning process that we will build on to in a diagram.

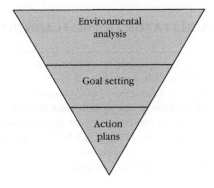

Fig. 3.1 The general planning process.

THE ANNUAL PLANNING TIMETABLE

For a key account to prosper, there needs to be an annual schedule of planning and forecasting activity. Table 3.1 is an example which you will need to modify to reflect your mix of accounts. In Table 3.1, the month refers to the month in the supplying company's financial year. I have assumed as a starting point that before the first event the team has updated its database of knowledge in the account. The team members understand the structure and know the key people they need to work with. The team further understands the financial position of the client and its goals and critical success factors. As has been said before, if this database of knowledge is poor, then the first planning session will be short and simply allocate tasks to the team to plug the knowledge gap.

I have also assumed that marketing strategies and other internal essential knowledge is available to the team. The length of the events are drawn from experience, but you will have to check their validity in your environment. Note that this table is for a key account manager. If there are more than one of these on the account, you will have to organize the sub-account planning session to coincide with or be compatible with this top level of planning.

For the shortened version the account manager would do those parts concerned with campaign plans and the annual sales operating plan. The resource requirement would in that case only come from the campaign plans.

USING A FACILITATOR IN THE PLANNING PROCESS

If the easy answer to the question "When should we use a formal planning process?" is "Whenever you need to," the easy answer to "When should we use a facilitator?" is "Whenever he or she can add value." It is hard to define a rule which states in what circumstances a facilitator would be appropriate. Account managers who understand how such sessions work are likely to get better at judging when it is appropriate to use the services of an outsider versed in the intricacies of team planning. Some guidelines are given below.

Table 3.1   An annual schedule of planning and forecasting activity.

Event	Document	Month	Comments
Annual planning event (3 days)	First draft of updated account plan. Includes a list of the likely key campaign plans	9	This event may or may not include the customer for, say, day one. If the customer attends more than the first day, the team may have to get together again to complete the more confidential part of the plan
			It is likely that the team will present the draft to a senior manager to ensure that its aspirations are consistent with the selling company's strategies, particularly on resources
Customer analysis validation	Updated account plan	10	The account manager will hold a series of meetings with the customer to validate and improve the customer analysis. I have assumed that it is not necessary to get the team together again to update the plan
Campaign planning	Campaign plans or updates of existing ones	10	Produces plans for the key sales campaigns highlighted in the account plan
Preparation of annual sales operating plan	Sales forecast Resource requirements	11	This shows the forecast for revenue and orders in detail for the next company year, and in outline for two further years

(continued overleaf)

Table 3.1 (*continued*).

Event	Document	Month	Comments
	Input to marketing		It also has the resource requirements for the account management objectives as well as the campaign plan activities. The resource requirements will include the need for senior managers to make sales calls in the account
Annual management review	Agreement to the resources requested or instructions to think again	12 or 1 in next year	NB make sure that everybody knows that this is a decision-making forum. If, on the other hand, management are not in a position to allocate resources, this must be made clear to everyone
Account team review (2 days)	Updates of account and campaign plans	3	An important review since it is not too late to make changes to ensure a successful year
Account team review (1 day)	Updated account and campaign plans	6	

Use a facilitator:

» when a significant number of members of the team are unfamiliar with the process;
» when an outsider's view may remove blockages to planning;
» when an outsider's view may help the team to raise its vision from the day-to-day problems of running the business;
» when an outsider's view may prevent the team ducking issues; or
» when an outsider's view may bring experience from similar planning sessions.

Do not use a facilitator:

» to handle issues which are straightforward people-management issues; or
» if the team is not serious about building a plan for which they intend to become accountable.

A facilitator from outside may bring the following benefits.

» *Organization*. An experienced facilitator will help with the set-up of the session and the accurate setting of expectations.
» *Guidance*. Previous experience allows the facilitator to guide the team through the process and look for shortcuts where possible.
» *Discipline*. An outside facilitator is in a good position to insist on the essential planning disciplines designed to ensure the efficiency of the session.
» *Vision*. An outsider, lacking the knowledge and prejudices of the planning team, can help to keep up the vision of the team, discover new creative ideas and foster a "can-do" team attitude. Facilitators who are working with many different companies gain an unusual insight into what is fashionable or what are the current trends and pressures in business generally.
» *Team building*. An outsider can assist with team building as an arbiter and asker of hard questions.
» *Adaptability*. If the facilitators are active with a number of teams they will be able to adapt the process and content of the sessions as market and internal company issues change.

At the end of the session the team will decide how to keep the process alive and if and how they wish to use the outside facilitation in the future.

SOME NOTES FOR FACILITATORS

Timing

The upside-down triangle (Fig. 3.1) tries to show diagrammatically the timing of a planning session. If it takes one unit of time to agree the goals, one hour, one day, one week, or whatever, it will take three to do the environmental analysis and about half a time unit to do the action plans.

Sales teams tend to be very activity-oriented and may find this process slightly laborious the first time through. During the environmental analysis they will see an awful lot of key issues which they know are going to lead to an awful lot of activity. They quite often feel a bit down at the end of the first day. Live with it. They will eventually get to goal setting and activity planning, and experience shows that the quality of the plan is directly related to the quality of the environmental analysis.

Remain flexible

To be frank it doesn't much matter if an issue is recorded as a weakness or a threat. As long as the issue is recorded it will impact on the plan, so do not be rigid. If you realize that the team is making a mistake, ask questions to enable them to see what is going wrong, but do not dwell on it.

Quite often poor sentences remain on the wall for a couple of days and then suddenly get corrected. We can always rectify mistakes later. Remember, it is their plan and they will be responsible for implementing it. The only person who doesn't need to be in 100% agreement with the plan is the facilitator.

The more plans the facilitator is involved in, however, the more ideas he or she will cross-fertilize into new plans. This is a good thing as it improves the quality of plans and saves time.

Teams with problems

If they are struggling, it is almost certainly because the previous element of the planning process has not been comprehensively or well done.

If they are having problems activity planning, maybe the goal is too broad or not specific enough. If they are having problems setting goals, it is probably because the S-SWOT is incomplete or rushed. If they are struggling with the S-SWOT, make them check the C-SWOT. If they are struggling with the C-SWOT, it is almost certainly because they do not have enough hard or soft data, i.e. they don't know enough about the customer. In such a case, curtail the planning session to a simple activity plan for finding out the necessary information.

Watch for low responders and very deliberately make them contribute. Watch for dominators and make them listen to the rest of the team. With the latter, it is sometimes necessary to have a word during a break.

Vision

Make them keep the vision up. If the plan is becoming unrealistic we will detect it at activity planning time and change it. Most plans err on the side of being highly achievable but not sufficiently stretching. The role of the facilitator is to balance that out.

KEY LEARNING POINTS

Organizing the team to handle a geographically spread key account requires good definition of roles and responsibilities within the team, the involvement of the whole team in planning the way forward, and systematic and regular planning and review sessions.

The E-Dimension
in Account Management

This chapter looks at the considerable opportunities that the e-dimension offers to account managers in two areas:

» information gathering; and
» training account teams.

THE E-DIMENSION – INFORMATION GATHERING

A professional account plan and its management starts from the strategic situation that customers find themselves in. The Internet offers the most convenient answer to the account manager's lament "We simply do not have the information about the customer that enables us to forecast where they might go and how we might help them."

So what does the team need? There are many factors that may affect the account team's performance. You need to study the economy carefully in countries where the customer is very active and superficially in other places. Most customer strategies depend to some extent on what is happening in the local as well as in the global economy. This research may be done from the home country of the team or, better, by local people in the actual geographic areas.

Get the team to look for issues that may have a radical impact first. For example, if you anticipate a fall in demand for the customer's products for economic reasons, note this, since it may determine into which parts of the customer organization you look for short-term sales. Alternatively, if your customer sells products to or provides a service for tourists, you will want to know the best predictions for the growth of tourism in their areas of operation. Note these economic trends and use the information later when forming action plans and allocating resources.

The dramatic pace of technological change has had an enormous impact on most organizations. The merging of communications techniques with computer information is steadily changing the way we all have to work and the way our customers have to work. Guard against any dangers or problems that new technology may introduce by discussing the latest relevant technological developments at your account planning meetings. If necessary, consult an expert or familiarize yourself with analysts' reports. Ask someone on the team to read the appropriate journals and give brief but concise updates to colleagues on a regular basis.

As an increasing number of organizations, particularly in the public sector, find themselves operating within regulatory frameworks, it is vital to understand exactly what the rules are. If you are selling to part of a government organization, you may have to take into account a change in the political party of the executive. In any case, you are subject to current employment laws which may have an impact on your strategic account plan in every country where you operate. Internal policy on intranet Websites may need to be made available to the team, or you may need to ask a legal adviser to help you with your fact-gathering. If you are not sure what data you need, brainstorm the possibilities with the team.

In all of this the Internet and intranet play hugely important roles.

THE E-DIMENSION IN ACCOUNT MANAGEMENT TRAINING

Recent trends in the business environment are driving significant changes in the way modern account managers operate. Like other managers they need to continuously challenge the way things are done and to find ways of improving. This is impacting on all aspects of account management, including the training and development of account teams.

The way account managers are expected to lead and manage is becoming fundamentally different – especially in situations where time and budget constraints are critical. Since they and team members must take greater responsibility for their own careers, there is also an increased focus on continuing personal development (CPD).

Many organizations are now adopting more of an integrated approach to account and team management training that breaks traditional methods into discrete activities that can then be supported through the desktop in the form of software tools. Five years ago few participants on public training programs wanted software to support application of the ideas back on the job – now an overwhelming majority have participants expecting software tools that reflect the newly acquired concepts! The implications to account management planning and control are significant where, for example, requests for tender documents received from customers require a consistent approach to the strategy of answering them and the tactics of the complex sales campaigns that follow.

In responding to the above challenges, account teams must address the following four phases of the overall development process.

1 *Assess.* What levels of capability do we need to deliver future account objectives and what have we got now?
2 *Build.* What is the most effective and efficient way to build competency in our teams – maximizing performance improvement?
3 *Sustain.* What is the best way to ensure that newly acquired concepts and methods are applied on-the-job in a consistent way that reflects "best practice?"
4 *Grow.* What is the best way of ensuring that teams learn from each other and from the past – creating a "continuous learning" culture without building long-term dependency on the trainer or consultant?

The starting point is to understand training and development needs in relation to the ability to deliver account targets. It there is no clear link between the development activity and business performance, then it has no value. Potential for the e-dimension: use online self-assessment checklists and development planners to support the concept of continuing personal development – *Don't view training and operations as disconnected.*

Once individual and team development needs have been identified, competencies can be developed in a number of ways. Traditionally this has been achieved using coaching or face-to-face workshops, but increasingly technology offers the potential to make training more cost effective and convenient to the learner. Potential for the e-dimension: make training available as and when required (JIT training) – *Don't throw account managers and their teams in at the deep end.*

Once new skills, such as account planning, have been acquired, it is essential that they be applied consistently and correctly over time. If there is no associated change in behavior, then there will be no impact on performance. An aspect of long-term memory, however, is that retention of new concepts and ideas falls off over time, and with it the confidence to apply new techniques. Due to the often restricted flexibility of training schedules, it is typically some time after a training event that the participant has an opportunity to use a new technique in anger. Potential for the e-dimension: use e-learning solutions and interactive tools to reinforce theory as and when concepts are applied in practice – *Don't start from a blank sheet of paper.*

Finally, whilst developing skills in an individual will affect their performance, this effect can be leveraged dramatically when all members of the team work to a common method using a common business language. Furthermore, the use of interactive templates that reflect the team's preferred way of working enables ideas and thoughts to be captured in a structured and consistent format, enabling members of remote teams to share their knowledge more effectively, and ensuring that when one member of the team leaves, their knowledge doesn't leave with them. Potential for the e-dimension: by using common electronic templates on a shared-access database, users can review and learn from the past and the work of others – *Don't re-invent the wheel.*

Fig. 4.1 illustrates how to sustain best practice.

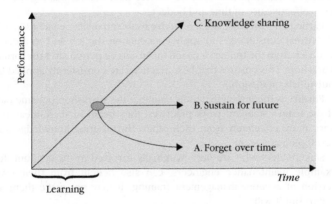

Fig. 4.1   The potential for the e-dimension.

In summary, the e-dimension can be used to combine best practice concepts and methods into a self-learning environment that supports the application of key account management methods on-the-job (moving from point A to point B in Fig. 4.1). Technology also provides a structured storage and easy retrieval system for an organization's accumulated knowledge (moving from point B to point C in

Fig. 4.1). It is this aspect that now allows continual account team-wide learning and knowledge management. You will find examples of these templates in Chapter 5 The Global Dimension in Account Management and Chapter 7 Account Management in Practice.

Here is a template for a "blended solution," face-to-face and electronic, to account management training.

Participants go on-line to review the course outline, read the basic concepts, and complete a quick self-assessment questionnaire, and are therefore better prepared for attending the workshop. Next, participants attend the face-to-face workshop (typically application-focused where ideas are applied to real job concerns – for example, working on a real account plan rather than a case study). However, the duration of these workshops will now be shorter than before, making them a more effective use of time and budget.

Participants then use the interactive tools and on-line coaches (a sort of "virtual consultant") to apply concepts on the job and to receive feedback from the trainer or coach for an agreed period after the formal workshop. This ensures that best practices are consistently applied by individuals on-the-job.

Finally, as the interactive tools taught at the workshop become part of the team's standard work practices, they begin to share ideas and learn more effectively from each other, thus sharing knowledge and developing as a team.

Stakeholders who are only marginally involved in the account, for example maintenance engineers, can also benefit from their own version of account management training. It may not make them an expert but it will:

» build awareness and competence;
» start to create a common business language;
» better prepare people for formal training if and when it does occur; and
» make them feel as though they have not been forgotten by the account manager or the team.

The addition of the e-dimension to global account management takes this topic another step forward in Chapter 5 The Global Dimension in Account Management.

KEY LEARNING POINTS

The Internet has removed any excuse an account team might offer for not having enough data on their customer and market to make a well-founded plan. The use of the Internet in training account teams is more cost effective than using only training events, and more likely to solve the problem of maintaining the good practice learnt in the classroom back on the job.

The Global Dimension in Account Management

This chapter considers the global dimension of account management in terms of:

» account management and global cultures;
» maintaining a global plan; and
» learning from other account managers.

ACCOUNT MANAGEMENT AND GLOBAL CULTURES

In a global environment the development of the international account manager has become a strategic activity. In developing truly international account managers, organizations are simultaneously fostering their own process of becoming international in outlook and practice. Central to this process is respect for, and awareness of, cultural diversity.

The successful international manager has to reconcile a number of key dilemmas which are common to all cultures. How do you expand the ethos and culture that has made the organization successful whilst recognizing that compromises have to be made to deal with local traditions and rules? Failure to reconcile these dilemmas will lead to the failure of an organization's international aspirations and strategies. Management in a global environment is increasingly affected by cultural differences. The way account management is deployed in a multicultural environment is, and needs to be, dependent on the broader strategy. It also reflects how truly international an organization is and, it is to be hoped, the level of internationalization of the corporation.

The international account manager needs to go beyond awareness of cultural differences. He or she needs to respect these differences and take advantage of diversity through reconciling cross-cultural dilemmas. The international account manager reconciles cultural dilemmas.

Basic to understanding other cultures is the awareness that culture is a series of rules and methods that a society has evolved to deal with the recurring problems it faces. They have become so basic that, like breathing, we no longer think about how we approach or resolve them. Every country and every organization faces dilemmas in relationships with people; dilemmas in relation to time; and dilemmas in relations between people and the natural environment. Culture is the way in which people resolve dilemmas emerging from universal problems. While nations differ markedly in how they approach these dilemmas, they do not differ in needing to make some kind of response. The successful international account manager is in a position to reconcile dilemmas more effectively by building a strategy that can be implemented consistently throughout the organization.

MAINTAINING A GLOBAL PLAN

E-learning is becoming an essential component of an organization's total development program because of its cost-effective nature and its reinforcement of ideas on-the-job. Organizations recognize that their real competitive advantage in key accounts lies in the combined knowledge and experience of their account managers and their teams. Account knowledge is now part of what is referred to as an organization's "intellectual capital." "Knowledge management" is the term used to describe getting the right information to the right people at the right time, and is quickly becoming a core competence of modern account management.

This is true from the information gathered about customers being available to all team members involved in the plan to simple things like a forum that all team members regularly access to keep up to date with the tactics the account manager is deploying. For example, "Team member A is going to visit the production manager at place X, is there anything other people want him to raise at that meeting." But the key to linking the activities of the whole account team on a global basis is the development of and access to the global account plan.

The chart shown in Fig. 5.1 is a template for account planning that, if made available to the worldwide team, can act as the bible for all action plans. Advice on completing the template and a case example is in Chapter 7 In Practice.

LEARNING FROM OTHER ACCOUNT MANAGERS

Without a systematic approach to the screening of new sales opportunities in a global account you will find the local salespeople going for everything – what is sometimes called the 'shotgun' approach. This may be successful for a while, but unfortunately it too often results in limited sales resources being spread too thinly across too many prospects, and the "best" prospects for sales not necessarily getting the right resource and focus.

The Opportunity Analyzer (see Fig. 5.2) ensures that the right opportunities are captured, prioritized, and acted upon by the team worldwide. Once again, loading this on the intranet means that the whole account team can contribute to the choice of projects to focus

ACCOUNT PLANNER		Name	
		Team	
		Date	
		Status	

	REFERENCE	COMPANY PROFILE
OVERVIEW	COMPANY NAME	
	MISSION STATEMENT	
	PRODUCTS & SERVICES	
	MARKETS & CUSTOMERS	
	OPERATIONAL PERFORMANCE	

	CUSTOMER STRENGTHS	I		CUSTOMER WEAKNESSES	I
CS1			CW1		
CS2			CW2		
CS3			CW3		
CS4			CW4		
CS5			CW5		
CS6			CW6		
CS7			CW7		
CS8			CW8		
CS9			CW9		
CS10			CW10		

	CUSTOMER OPPORTUNITIES	I		CUSTOMER THREATS	I
CO1			CT1		
CO2			CT2		
CO3			CT3		
CO4			CT4		
CO5			CT5		
CO6			CT6		
CO7			CT7		
CO8			CT8		
CO9			CT9		
CO10			CT10		

(left margin: MARKET ATTRACTIVENESS)

Acc Man figures.xls Page 1 of 3

Fig. 5.1 Account planning.

		TITLE	DESCRIPTION		OWNER	DATE	VALUE	S
TOP TEN SALES CAMPAIGNS	SC1							
	SC2							
	SC3							
	SC4							
	SC5							
	SC6							
	SC7							
	SC8							
	SC9							
	SC10							

		OUR STRENGTHS	I	G		OUR WEAKNESSES	I	G
	OS1				OW1			
	OS2				OW2			
	OS3				OW3			
	OS4				OW4			
	OS5				OW5			
	OS6				OW6			
	OS7				OW7			
	OS8				OW8			
	OS9				OW9			
	OS10				OW10			

		OUR OPPORTUNITIES	I	G		OUR THREATS	I	G
CUSTOMER ATTRACTIVENESS	OO1				OT1			
	OO2				OT2			
	OO3				OT3			
	OO4				OT4			
	OO5				OT5			
	OO6				OT6			
	OO7				OT7			
	OO8				OT8			
	OO9				OT9			
	OO10				OT10			

Fig. 5.1 (*continued*)

	ACCOUNT READINESS GROUPS	S	SPIDER'S WEB
READINESS	G1 LEVEL OF CONTACT		
	G2 CUSTOMER SATISFACTION		
	G3 ACCOUNT PLANNING		
	G4 COMPETITIVE POSITION		
	G5 STRATEGIC PRODUCTS & SERVICES		
	G6 KEY CUSTOMER STRATEGIES		
	G7 PIPELINE		
	G8 MARKET SHARE		

	OBJECTIVES	G	INDICATOR	OWNER	DATE	S
ACCOUNT OBJECTIVES	O1					
	O2					
	O3					
	O4					
	O5					
	O6					
	O7					
	O8					
	O9					
	O10					
	O11					
	O12					
	O13					
	O14					
	O15					

	ITEM	RESOURCE REQUIREMENTS TO IMPLEMENT THE PLAN	BUDGET	S
RESOURCES	PEOPLE			
	FACILITIES			
	EQUIPMENT			
	MATERIALS			
		TOTAL BUDGET	£0.00	

Fig. 5.1 (*continued*)

OPPORTUNITY ANALYZER

Name	
Team	
Date	
Status	

TITLE

OPPORTUNITY

PM Focus	Name	PM Group	
Customer			
Product			

Value	Worst case	Expected	Best case
Typical margin (%)			
Annual revenues			
One-off costs			
On-going costs			£0
Total costs	£0	£0	£0

£1
£1
£1
£0
£0
£0

Pessimistic   Mean   Optimistic

Annual revenues — One-off costs
On-going costs   Total costs

SWOT

Criteria	Strengths, Weaknesses, Opportunities & Threats
Strengths	
Weaknesses	
Opportunities	

STRATEGIC FIT

Criteria	Strategic analysis	
Impact on competition		
Suitable		
Acceptable		
Feasible		

Decision	Reason for decision

Fig. 5.2 The Opportunity Analyzer.

on, and they can learn from each other about new opportunities they did not realize were there, or how to sell current projects using the weight of the global approach. Besides which, there is rarely enough time or sufficient resource to address all new sales opportunities.

Conducting a full business case on all new opportunities can take too long and feel bureaucratic to the team. It also delays the overall process. New opportunities should initially be quantified in terms of their potential impact on bottom line sales and margin. Priority should be given to opportunities where there is a strong probability of success and where there is a clear fit with the account manager's competitive strategy.

Here is how to complete the opportunity analyzer.

Opportunity

» What is the name of the customer, and what is the name of the product or service opportunity?
» What is the product-market (PM) group that the customer and product belong to? (Note: these groups may be defined in the company's strategy or marketing plan.)
» Is the opportunity related to a current (C), modified (M), or new (N) product and customer? (Note: for new products and customers, greater work is often needed for a successful sale.)
» What are the forecast revenues and costs for this opportunity? (Notes: 1 one-off costs include all activities prior to and during the sales campaign; 2 ongoing costs are incurred to maintain and support the sale.)

SWOT

Strengths, weaknesses, opportunities, and threats.

» What are our strengths and weaknesses in trying to close this sale?
» What are the opportunities and threats we face if we proceed with this sales opportunity?

(Note: ensure that the stated strengths and weaknesses relate to this specific campaign.)

Strategic fit

How does this opportunity perform against each of the criteria used to test strategic fit?

» Suitable = is it consistent with the strategy and the current situation?
» Acceptable = will it be acceptable to all key stakeholders?
» Feasible = will it be feasible given time and resource constraints?
» Enduring = will this opportunity present long-term benefits as well as a short-term gain?

An international account manager should get each of their salespeople in the geographic territories to go through an exercise like this for each opportunity they are going after. That way they are focusing on the best opportunities and maximizing the return from the account. As with the account plan, making the results available on the company intranet completes the learning exercise.

KEY LEARNING POINTS

Account managers are as responsible as any other international manager for arriving at a synergy between the values and culture at the home of the company with the values and culture in the overseas locations they spread to. It is vital to allow wide access to account plans so that they remain acceptable to all concerned and allow teams to learn from other people.

The State of the Art in Account Management

This chapter looks at the elements involved in creating a team-built account plan:

» producing a plan to ensure the long-term relationship with the key account;
» the creative planning process and the database of knowledge;
» SWOT analysis, goal setting, and activity planning;
» resource planning and allocation; and
» groundrules of planning and suggested timetables.

OBJECTIVES OF A KEY ACCOUNT PLANNING SESSION

A planning session starts from a vision or mission. We want to change, possibly dramatically, a part of the world to our vision of it. The mission could be very broad or very focused, but it gives the starting point of the plan.

The objective of a planning session is "To produce the best possible plan to achieve this mission." Notice how the objective breaks the rules of normal objectives – "best possible" is not an accurate measurement for achievement. We have to accept this, though, as a more accurate test for success could constrain the creative thinking of the plan. If, for example, the team set a mission "To capture 50% of the addressable market," it would have two problems. How does it know before the planning process that this is achievable, and how does it know that if it tried it could not achieve more?

EXAMPLE OF A PLANNING TEAM'S MISSION STATEMENTS

We wish to produce the best possible plan to achieve our mission:

» to be the supplier of first choice to the account in all of Europe and North America;
» to be and to be seen to be a major supplier in the civil government market;
» to improve our market share in the account worldwide;
» to achieve at least 10% higher level of revenue growth in the account every year for the next 3 years; and
» to use our reputation in the pharmaceuticals division of the account to gain 10% of the orders placed in the chemicals division within a year.

WHO IS THERE?

In this section we will limit ourselves to a key account team planning session. An example of the people involved is:

» account manager, account consultant, services consultant;
» any other cross-functional account teams dedicated to parts of the account;
» an appropriate marketing person; and
» appropriate sub-accountees (we will use the term "sub-accountee" to describe an account manager or salesperson responsible for part of the account).

It is likely that the team will comprise between six and eight people. If it is the first time for the team, the session will probably last at least three days. If there is a facilitator, he or she will be responsible for describing and getting agreement to the groundrules of planning. He or she will also police and time the session to ensure that by the end the team has reached an appropriate point in the process.

It is highly desirable to have a senior manager attend the last session of the key account planning event to hear a short presentation of the team's conclusions. This gives a focus to the team, who will have to be ready to make such a presentation when the time comes.

HOW LONG DO YOU WORK?

Experience shows that after eight or nine hours the productivity of planners drops dramatically. It is probably better, therefore, to finish at around 17.30. If it is a new team or some new members are joining, it is a good idea to have the meeting off-site and to have dinner together. Don't forget, though, you are trying to make these planning events regular and routine. It is a good idea to call a one- or two-day planning session to modify a particular part of the plan and to hold such a meeting in an ordinary conference room.

WHAT DO YOU NEED?

The only documentation you need will be incorporated on flipcharts by the end of the session. So, make sure you supply:

» two flipchart stands;
» many pads of flipchart paper; and
» flipchart pens with at least the colors blue, red, green, and black.

Set the chairs, as comfortably as possible, in a semicircle facing the flipcharts and the facilitator. Discourage tables and notepads.

THE KEY ACCOUNT PLAN OUTLINE DESCRIPTION

The account plan upside-down triangle is shown in Fig. 6.1. In trying to explain the upside-down triangle we will start from an overview, and discuss each element in more detail later. The headings for the description are:

» the creative planning process
» database of knowledge
» SWOT analysis
» goal setting
» activity planning
» resource plan
» resource allocation
» groundrules of planning.

The creative planning process

The word "creative" reminds us that we are looking for the best possible plan. Try to avoid all your prejudices and preconceived ideas. In particular, in the early part of the planning process we will not constrain our thinking by doubts about the availability of resources. We will of course recognize that there is a management budgeting cycle and that our plan needs to have resources approved at appropriate times during that cycle. Nevertheless we need creative ideas to generate new initiatives. After all, any company's management can put resource where they like. If we give management a good business case and enough time to react, they can resource any project that we could exploit.

HIGH HOPES IN AEROSPACE

A team was preparing an account plan for an aircraft manufacturer. It considered the strong position it had built and was agonizing over what the short- to medium-term aspiration for market share should be.

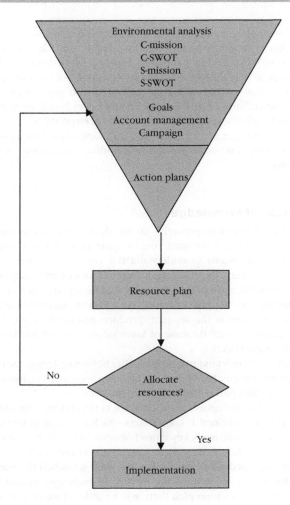

Fig. 6.1 Account plan outline.

At one point a junior member of the team said that the logic of the plan so far led to the fact that the account team's goal should be for 100% of all large computers supplied. At first rejected by the team as unrealistic, the members were slowly won over until that goal was set. They achieved customer board approval of this some nine months later. The single vendor policy lasted two years, during which the account team's order book swelled.

The team learnt good lessons from this, particularly that anyone in the team can make significant contributions through new insights.

Database of knowledge

Remember the Chinese proverb – do not decide where you want to go and how to get there until you are quite certain where you are now. The team needs to understand the customer's business, the customer's industry, the customer's current financial and competitive environment, the influences of the general economy, etc. That's before the team adds the supplier company environment, its current market strategies, position in the account, products and services, etc. If we have organized a huge database of knowledge, planning will become more and more effective.

For the moment let us imagine that either before, or during, the event the account manager has briefed the planning team on the information necessary to take part in the creation of the plan.

It is useful to distinguish in the database between hard data and soft data. Hard data is defined as known facts which are normally historical. What were the customer's key ratios last year? How did they compare with the competition? How many employees do they have and how are they organized? And that list has not even scratched the surface. The team will never have all the facts at its fingertips. Indeed, in a new account penetration plan there will be little information to hand and the planning session will be quite short, but the more information available to the team the better.

Soft data is in many ways as important or even more important than hard data. It includes all the prejudices and politics of the people side of the business. This data consists of the subjective opinions drawn by customer managers or the account team.

DO NOT TAKE THINGS AT FACE VALUE

In any large company there is an organization chart. It is hard data. It says: "That person reports to that person, who reports to that person, who reports to that person, etc." The soft data asks "Yes, but who actually runs the business, who has influence, who can make things happen and, equally, who can stop things happening?"

In many large British companies there is a network of people with similar backgrounds who, though in different divisions and at different levels in the business, form a powerful *virtual team*. In one very large business in the UK the organization chart did not reveal – without further examination – the fact that many established and up and coming executives had not only attended the same university, but also the same college within that university.

The environment section of a creative planning process includes the background knowledge, including the soft data brought by everyone in the team.

SWOT analysis

The analysis technique which we use for sorting out our knowledge and different team members' angles on the plan is called SWOT analysis – Strengths, Weaknesses, Opportunities, and Threats. This is a simple technique, as so many good ones are, for helping the team to understand what it needs to do in the account. Unfortunately, like all techniques it can be implemented well or badly. Further guidance on good SWOT analysis follows, so suffice it to say at this point that a comprehensive, well-documented SWOT analysis makes the next part of the planning process reasonably straightforward.

The objective of SWOT analysis is not simply to describe the environment, rather it is to describe the environment in a way which helps us to understand what we need to do. It is in two parts, the customer SWOT (C-SWOT) and the supplier SWOT (S-SWOT). Once we have got an agreed description of the environment we can decide what to do about it.

Goal setting

Following the use of a bridging technique which ensures that the work done in the SWOT analysis is fully exploited, the team sets its goals. In a key account plan goals are divided into account management goals and campaign goals.

Account management goals are the relationship goals and tend to be more strategic and longer term than campaign goals. Experience has enabled us to break down account management goals into eight goal areas. Not all plans will require goals in all eight areas, but all plans will require goals in some of these areas. The detail of this follows, but for the sake of example, three of these goal areas are:

» level of contact
» customer satisfaction
» market share.

Campaign goals are goals where a major milestone is taking an order from a customer for the supplier's products and/or services. It is likely that campaign goals will be "owned" by a sub-accountee or the salesperson responsible for the campaign rather than the account manager. The methods used for campaign planning are explained in *ExpressExec* – Complex Sales Planning.

Having decided what we want to achieve, we come to the last part of the planning process – the activity plans.

Activity planning

It is very much a personal decision as to the amount of detail into which activity plans have to go. Some people are comfortable with quite macro actions and milestones which are weeks or even months apart. Other people try to plan all the activities required to achieve the goal in the minutest detail, even down to a telephone call. It is personal preference. Either will do as long as it achieves the aim of activity planning, which is to estimate the resources required to achieve the goal.

The team should now be in a position to produce its best forecast of its achievements in the account, both short-term and long-term, and the amount of resource investment required from the supplying company to achieve these results.

Resource plan

The resource plan is actually a re-sort of the activity plan. If we know what has to be done and who has to do it, we can produce our best estimate of the resources required. This enables us to move to the next step in the planning process. This is either part of the normal budgeting cycle or, on some occasions, a special case to take to management as a long- or short-term business investment plan.

It is vital to narrow down an accurate definition of the resources which will be needed to implement the plan. Too often the team starts to implement the early part of the plan, only to find a resource problem later. The team needs to get itself into good order to move to the next step, which is to persuade management to put those resources at the team's disposal.

Resource allocation

Most account plans require resources which are not in the direct control of the account team. A decision box occurs, therefore, when management decide on the merits of the various plans being put forward and allocate their resources.

We should try to see this as a contract. The account team is saying to the appropriate level of management "I will give you these results," meaning the goals, "if you will give me these resources." If management say "yes," either immediately or as the budgeting cycle grinds on, the team implements the plan. If management say "no," the team adjusts its goals and resubmits, because, of course, no planning process is complete until the resources have been allocated to its implementation. Be careful. Management can often, from their wider experience, offer shortcuts towards account teams' goals and therefore legitimately reduce the amount of resource required to achieve the result.

However, in an immature planning cycle, management, particularly sales management, have a habit of liking the sound of the result, but not allocating the resource in full. At worst, this leads to teams second guessing the likelihood of their getting resources when they are setting goals and completely constrains the creativity of the plan. For their part, account teams must recognize that although management can get any resource required to achieve a well-constructed business plan, it requires more than a week's notice. The plans must signal in detail this year's resource requirement and broadly the requirement of the subsequent two years, particularly if special or unusual resources are going to be required.

In this opening we have looked in outline at the key account planning process. More detail on each element follows a statement on the disciplines required from the planning team during the process.

Groundrules of planning

The groundrules are concerned with the efficiency of the planning session. Where two or three people are gathered together, you will find differences of opinion, multiple ideas, different angles on the same topic, personal prejudices, and all the other features of a team of human beings. These tend to reduce the efficiency of a team. It is the job of the facilitator, and of course of the team itself, to maintain a number of disciplines.

1 *Talk and document in short, simple but complete sentences.* This item is proved in the detail on SWOT analysis, and is probably the most important rule. If we talk in bullet points then we will get quick agreement to a rough definition of the key issues. But what we need is the agreement of the team to a detailed statement of the *real meaning* of the key issue.

2 *Equal voice/equal vote.* In a creative planning session, rank disappears. It is vital that the planning team does not believe that it is there to wait until the senior person has expressed a view and then agree with it. Real creativity may easily come from a member of the team who is the most junior and therefore the least experienced. So, account managers, a sure way to kill the creativity of your team is to make it plain, after about an hour of planning, that the only plan which is going to be acceptable is the one you had in your head before the meeting started. Remember that to get a team committed

to a plan of action you must encourage it to take part in the planning process. Avoid telling them what they are going to do, like a prophet with tablets of stone. In the end, however, the team has to get to a plan.

The difference between equal voice and equal vote is best shown by an example. In a discussion about where to go on holiday children have an equal voice, they can say where they want to go, but they certainly don't have a vote. The account manager's neck is on the block, so in extreme cases he or she may have to use some assertiveness to get to a satisfactory conclusion.

In practice there are rarely problems in this area. The team is pleased to be part of the planning process and will normally get amicably to the necessary consensus.

3 *One hundred percent agreement*. Allied to the above is the rule of 100% agreement. Read literally this means that no part of the plan is firm until all members of the team have agreed with it. It is important. Most planning sessions produce new directions and new activities for all of the members of the team. In many cases these will be in addition to or different than the activities which the team member has under way. If the momentum of the plan is to be kept up and the new directions implemented, it is vital that everyone agrees and that the timescales and resources have been accurately forecast.

If this rule goes wrong, you will find that people are not disagreeing with a part of the plan simply because they have, in fact, no intention of carrying out their role in it: "They can write it up if they want, it ain't going to happen."

4 *Do not duck issues*. Following on the 100% agreement, a successful planning session tables and discusses all the key issues surrounding the plan. Here are some examples of issues which are frequently ducked:

» a person agrees to an activity, but team members do not believe he or she has the necessary knowledge or skills to carry it out;
» a necessary activity is in someone else's province and we duck the issue of how to get that person's support for the plan;
» an activity is agreed which has a dependency on higher management agreement and no plan is put in place to gain this; and

» an activity is agreed which has a dependency on the customer's part and no plan is put in place to ensure that the customer can and does achieve the dependency.

5 *Think before you speak.* Do not keep too rigidly to this because sometimes people do think through an idea while they are articulating it. But it is a useful rule to agree before the planning session starts so that we can use it to muffle someone who frequently waffles.

The facilitator will present these rules to the team and, given that they agree to abide by them, the planning session proper can begin.

SUGGESTED TIMETABLES FOR PLANNING MEETINGS

Some of the following sessions are dealt with more fully in Chapter 10 Ten Steps to Implementing Account Management.

Creating a new plan or the annual planning review

» **Session:** an initial meeting to create a new plan or complete a major annual review.
» **Delegates:**

   » the worldwide team brought together for the annual event;
   » marketing representatives; and
   » the customer, for the customer environmental analysis.

» **Objective:** to produce the best possible plan to attain a mission statement or achieve an objective.
» **Timescale:** three days.
» **Timetable:** see Table 6.1.

Reviewing an account plan

Once an account team has produced an account plan and agreed with senior management that it should be implemented, the reviewing of that plan is strongly analogous to a meeting of a board of directors. Such a team must meet monthly or quarterly to agree progress on the plan, take remedial action where required, and then consider the longer term

Table 6.1   Timetable for creating a new plan.

Timetable Day 1

9.00	Introduction to the planning process by the facilitator and team agreement to the process and disciplines
9.40	Agreement to the S-mission statement or the objective which acts as the scope of the planning session
10.00	Definition of the C-mission
10.30	Coffee
10.45	C-SWOT analysis to identify the strengths and weaknesses of the customer in striving to achieve the C-mission
12.30	Lunch
1.30	C-SWOT analysis (continued)
3.30	Coffee
3.45	Start of S-SWOT to identify the supplying company's strengths and weaknesses in striving to achieve the S-mission
5.30	End of session

Timetable Day 2

9.00	S-SWOT (continued)
10.30	Coffee
11.45	S-SWOT (continued)
12.30	Lunch
1.30	S-SWOT (continued)
3.30	Coffee
3.45	Facilitator presents and presides over the C-SWOT to S-SWOT check and the creation of the control matrix and spider's web (see Chapter 10)
4.30	Facilitator presents rules for setting goals and action plans with accountability
4.45	Goal setting – account management goals
6.30	End of session

Timetable Day 3

9.00	Goal setting – account management goals (continued) and campaign goals

(continued overleaf)

Table 6.1   (*continued*)

10.30	Coffee
10.45	Goal setting (continued)
11.45	Split into relevant teams to plan activities
12.30	Lunch
1.30	Activity planning
3.30	Coffee
3.45	Activity planning (continued)
5.00	Presentation to senior manager of the plan so far
6.30	End of session

issues which may alter current strategy or offer new opportunities. The objective is to amend the plan in accordance with achievements to date and changes in the environment.

The review process

» **Timescale:** maximum one day.
» **Agenda:** prior to the meeting, each "owner" of a goal should submit to the administrator a note of progress towards their account management and campaign goals. These should be circulated along with a statement of the issues to be discussed in the afternoon session.

Morning: each campaign goal "owner" should briefly introduce progress to date and suggest amendments. The account team discusses and agrees changes to the plan, particularly agreeing new actions to overcome obstacles which are proving difficult to remove.

Afternoon: the afternoon is kept for longer term issues. It is vital that the operational problems discussed in the morning session do not overflow into the afternoon and stop the "board" from assessing new opportunities and looking ahead.

The team should consider:
» amendments to the associated SWOT analysis;
» issues requiring remedial actions; and
» recommendations for decisions.

» **The facilitator:** the facilitator is a useful person in such a meeting and has a role very similar to a non-executive "director." Where the account team, for example, might duck an issue which is difficult to resolve the facilitator will intervene. The facilitator is important in maintaining good planning disciplines.

Some issues in the afternoon session may be large enough to require the statement of a mission or aiming focus, followed by a SWOT analysis and the setting of goals and action plans in the usual way. At this stage, the team may realize that the problem or opportunity under discussion needs more time or a different natural planning team. In this case the action plan will be to hold a planning session for the appropriate people for a suitable time. It is at the afternoon session that the team could invite other speakers to present to them on new or changing parts of the business environment.

KEY LEARNING POINTS

Account planning is best done by a team working creatively together. It is vital to obey the rules and follow the process of a planning session in a way that does not cause the team to spend a lot of time on semantics, or feel inhibited in their suggestions and ideas.

Account Management
in Practice

In this chapter we look at best practice by:

» studying examples of good account planning technique;
» looking at a complete example at the end of the process; and
» explaining the headings involved in the step-by-step planning process.

INTRODUCTION

Every account plan is, by its definition, individual to the industry sectors and nature of the supplier's and the customer's business. Perhaps we can learn most, therefore, by looking at a series of examples of good practice statements at each stage of the account planning process. We will do this, and then give a full example of a company that sells food products to supermarkets. (Note: remember that SWOT analysis stands for strengths, weaknesses, opportunities, and threats.) See Fig. 7.1.

EXAMPLES

Examples of mission statements

Here are some examples of practical customer mission statements:

» a major American bank has the mission statement: "To be the best financial services provider in the world;"
» a UK police force: "To be the envy of every other force in the country;" and
» the AA in the UK: "To be the UK's leading and most successful personal assistance organization."

If the planning team chooses such a broad mission as the driver of the planning session, it will take a very comprehensive view of the account.

Here are some examples of mission statements which are more limited in their scope:

» C-mission for a telecommunication company: "To reduce our dependency on BT by achieving one sale to Mercury by end December 1990;" and
» a food manufacturer: "To continue our rapid growth of business in Russia."

In both cases these are pretty focused C-missions leading to activities which are channeled into one particular issue in the account.

Below are some examples of good customer SWOT statements.

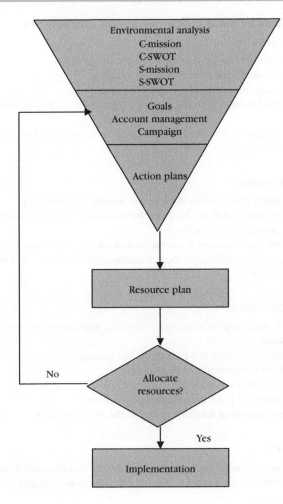

Fig. 7.1 Account plan outline.

Examples of good customer SWOT statements

C-strengths

» The customer has the technical resources and skills.
» The necessary investment money is available.
» Top management is committed to the mission.
» They can leverage from the reputation gained in their large installed base.
» The company is represented in all the parts of the world on which it wishes to focus.

C-weaknesses

» Some aging plant cannot achieve the required productivity.
» Some managers will not agree to the changes to their jobs necessary if the mission is to be achieved.
» Some managers cannot learn the new skills which are necessary.
» We cannot expand department X because there is no pool of skilled labor available.

C-opportunities

» Gather marketing information on pricing, potential customers, and competition.
» Change the career paths for key middle managers.
» Invest in communications technology.
» Sell the chemicals division.
» Re-engineer all the current business processes.
» Delegate industrial relations policy to the business units.

C-threats

» If top management do not settle the working practices and demarcation problems we cannot achieve the productivity required to meet the mission.
» If the price of oil rises above $40 per barrel the profitability aim is not achievable.
» If the government privatizes electricity generation, our current sales structure will become ineffective.

» If we fail to achieve the productivity aims in the mission statement, top management will invest elsewhere.
» The competition could catch up with our product advantage.

Now we move on to the supplier mission statements and SWOT analysis.

Examples of practical supplier mission statements

» To be acknowledged as the natural choice for our type of products and services.
» To improve our market share in chemicals division.
» To break into the commercial department for the first time by proving that investment in our products and services will assist the department in its productivity targets.
» To optimize our sales during this company year.
» To be the leading supplier in the account.

Examples of good supplier SWOT statements

S-strengths

» If we have good reason, it is simple for us to gain access to senior management and keep our information up to date.
» Our position as market leader means that we already have the necessary credibility to provide major solutions.
» We can mirror the global organization of the customer.
» The company is prepared to work with small and therefore flexible suppliers.

S-weaknesses

» We have less senior management contact than our principal competitor.
» The current product is not as usable as the one planned for launch in three months.
» The north-west region has had an interrupted delivery pattern.
» Our senior management have not agreed that the customer should be a special case for early product launch.

S-opportunities

» Organize a joint planning session.
» Run a series of road shows to enable the director of telecommunications to keep the people in the divisions up to date.
» Sell a consultancy project to report on the feasibility of a call center approach.

S-threats

» The customer board could decide it is too dependent on our products and services and encourage competition to win some market share.
» The part of the business where we are strong could be sold.
» All the work we are doing at technical level could be invalidated by a board decision to invest elsewhere.

Example of the link between the environmental analysis and goal setting

Figure 7.2 is an example of the radar diagram that represents the position that Universal Systems Integration starts from, with the explanation of how it defined the parameters. Universal Systems Integration has sold technical computers into a number of divisions of a large corporation. However, one large division is a recent acquisition to the group and is a heavy Universal user for commercial and technical applications.

We recently bid for and won a contract to supply the hardware and software for the building of a communications network. The spider's web is explained like this.

» Level of contact – score 3.
   We have never spoken to top management at corporate level. In the division where we are strong we have slumped to an IT only contact with the division's general manager meeting us socially from time to time.
» Customer satisfaction/Universal contribution – score 6.
   We have performed well and score highly on the customer satisfaction survey. However, we do not know if the customer measures RoI before or after investment. We are not sure either what the network is supposed to achieve for the business, beyond "we need to be able to talk to each other."

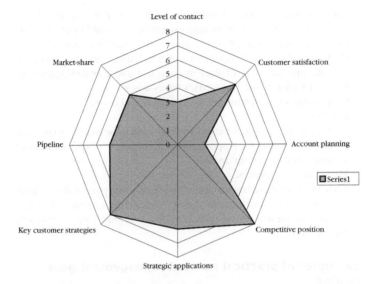

Fig. 7.2 A radar diagram for Universal Systems Integration.

» Account planning – score 2.

We have hardly started this and are blocked from getting the process going by our poor level of contact.

» Competitive position – score 8.

It would take a very long time indeed to get rid of the Universal installed base. Our position as the network supplier will tend to give us early warning of future bids.

» Strategic applications, products, and services – score 6.

The leverage from the network is crucial for us, the network crucial for the customer. We do not really know how to exploit this.

» Key customer strategies – score 7.

The network-oriented approach should prove suitable for the customer's business strategy of export-led market growth. There is an agreed and recent IT strategy at board level; but it is not well sold to the divisions. Its decentralized tone should suit us, but we are not really involved in discussing the long term. The customer has a problem with the role of its long-established central IT department. Its rather autocratic approach could conflict with the new strategy for IT. They still tend to believe that a user initiative out in the divisions to make investment is a failure in central IT and an extravagance on the user's part. If the role carries on as it is we will continue to be kept at arm's length from senior managers and users.

» Pipeline – score 5.

Our pipeline is not sufficient to reflect our new market share. We do not understand the opportunities at corporate or divisional level outside our own strong division.

» Market share – score 5.

Our market share has just increased significantly and will continue to do so in the short term as the network is implemented. The key to maintaining that momentum is to discover more opportunities in the pipeline.

Examples of practical account management goal setting

Taking this spider's web the team is able to look first at the priority areas, which are the points on which it scores lowest. It makes sense therefore for the team to spend the start of the goal-setting session agreeing what to do in the areas of:

» level of contact
» account planning
» pipeline.

Examples of level of contact goals

You have to find a wording for the goal which is satisfactory for the whole team to buy into. It must not look impossible or as though it will fail at the first hurdle. On the other hand, it must be stretching enough to be worth the effort which the team is going to put into it.

In terms of measurability, again, different teams will be comfortable with different types of goal. They may be quite happy with one that is a measure of quality which they can review and in which they can notice improvement. In this case the goal will end up something like this:

> To establish sustainable business relationships with heads of business units, main board directors and IT directors by the end of our next financial year.

Inside that goal the team then agrees activities which will move it in the direction of the goal. If you like, the measurable part of the goal is contained in the next level of the plan – the activity plan.

Another team will prefer to build into the goal specific actions which will measure whether or not there is an improvement in the information database as a result of raising the level of contact. In this case the goal would be more like:

> Within six months to have met with the members of the corporate policy and resources committee and with each general manager and financial controller of the four divisions.
>
> In each meeting to determine their business goals, strategies and critical success factors.

Notice how this goal is in two sentences. The plan may look more elegant if each goal is written in one sentence, but elegance is not the point. The team is trying to agree goals which it will then, over a period of time, try to achieve. If it feels comfortable with what is above, then so be it.

Neither of these goals flawlessly follow the strict definition of perfectly set objectives, but both were good enough for a team to change its level of contact dramatically.

Examples of account planning goals

Again, the team has two basic possibilities here. It is probably better if it can agree a long-term goal in this area with a good action plan to demonstrate that it knows how it is going to be achieved. Such a goal would look like this:

Within 18 months to have held a joint planning session with at least two divisional management teams and the corporate policy and resources committee.

The team should remember that it does not have to be a fully fledged three-day planning session in the first place. It may be more achievable to limit the aspiration to a one-day session where there is a well thought out and agreed agenda, driven by the account team.

It may be more important at this time to concentrate on an internal goal, particularly if the team or the account is new. In this case the team may decide to look at roles and responsibilities internally.

To build a focused global team with defined roles, responsibilities, and communications processes in place by the end of the calendar year. To agree these with the appropriate managers prior to the definition of next year's targets.

Examples of pipeline goals

Pipeline goals tend to be the most quantifiable of the account management goals. After all, basic selling technique tells us to understand what our hit rate is in turning prospects into orders. We know the order target, either because it is given to us by management or because it is driven by the market-share goal. From that and the picture of the current pipeline we can calculate what we have to identify. You also need to take into account the selling cycle. If it takes on average three months to take an opportunity from discovery to fruition, then that also helps to dictate what amount of pipeline is needed and when. Table 7.1 gives an example of calculating the pipeline requirement. This would lead to a pipeline goal as follows:

By three-quarters of the way through the company year to have identified new potential orders to the value of £3,500,000.

All the sub-account managers would then take their share of this prospecting job in their parts of the account. In this way the team has addressed the key weakness areas discovered in the environmental analysis.

Table 7.1 Calculating the pipeline requirement.

Total market next year	£10,000,000
Market share required	25%
Orders needed this year	£2,500,000
Normal hit rate	One success in two campaigns
Pipeline required	£5,000,000
Current pipeline	£1,500,000
Shortfall	£3,500,000

Further examples of account management goals

To perform consistently to agreed standards of service, network performance, and communications (e.g. every letter answered within 24 hours) by a date agreed with the customer in discussions about the benchmarks for this goal.

Measuring customer satisfaction by criteria agreed specifically with the account itself is always preferable to using generalized customer surveys.

To demonstrate our capability to match our services to the company's business objectives.

This is a good objective for a team which is going to try to demonstrate a particularly good "fit" between the two companies. International spread is frequently a feature of this sort of strategy.

To achieve year on year growth in both revenue and addressable market share.

This objective is more to do with protection from the competition than with the annual sales targets, which will still need to be defined. Many teams have complained that it is not possible to measure market share in a key account. This is either because there are simply too many units out there to count, or because they claim that no two suppliers are selling into exactly the same "market." I tend to push back on this by pointing out that it is not a mathematically accurate process. What we need is a rough idea of our share which we can then use subsequently as a base point for measuring the trend.

Figure. 7.3 shows how a food products supplier has documented its account plan for a key supermarket account. The process by which the planning got there is given below. This is the documentation available through *ExpressExec* in electronic form. Go to our website ExpressExec.com for details.

The overview below offers an explanation of the process the team has gone through to get this result. The "bible" of the account manager is the account plan. The actions on it dictate how the supplying teams approach the customer. The account plan includes a comprehensive statement of the situation at the supplier. It sets out the short- and long-term goals, and includes an action plan that, when implemented, will make sales easier to achieve, and more profitable. A more detailed statement of the logistical exercise and how to go through it is in Chapter 10 Ten Steps to Implementing Account Management.

OVERVIEW
Supplier mission statement

A planning session starts from a vision or mission. We want to change, possibly dramatically, a part of the world to our vision of it. The mission could be very broad or very focused; but it gives the starting point of the plan. The mission statement might be fairly concrete in terms of market share or sales targets, fairly intangible (such as to be seen to be a major supplier in a particular market), or quite short term (such as to make a first sale to a new account). The objective of a planning session is "To produce the best possible plan to achieve this mission." Notice how the objective breaks the rules of normal objectives – "best possible" is not an accurate measurement for achievement. We have to accept this, though, as a more accurate test for success could constrain the creative thinking of the plan.

Products and services

Summarize the products and services that the customer company takes to market.

ACCOUNT PLANNER

Name	
Team	
Date	
Status	

OVERVIEW

REFERENCE	COMPANY PROFILE
COMPANY NAME	Ace Supermarkets
MISSION STATEMENT	
PRODUCTS & SERVICES	entertainment products.
MARKETS & CUSTOMERS	Ace reach their customers through very large hypermarkets, normal size High Street supermarkets and small Ace Fast stores where these are appropriate to the community.
OPERATIONAL PERFORMANCE	Ace has recently invested £1 billion in new stores, whilst at all times making profits at about the industry average despite a lower gross margin because of their pricing policy.

	CUSTOMER STRENGTHS	I	GROUP		CUSTOMER WEAKNESSES	I	GROUP
CS1	Reputation for keen prices	7		CW1	Very low gross margin	7	
CS2	The range of designer clothes connected to a major design name	7		CW2	Reputation with 'professionals' as down market stores	5	
CS3	Food and non-food brands with a European connection	5		CW3	Low paid staff give 'cheap and cheerful' service	8	
CS4	Reputation as a contributor to the local community	3		CW4	Size of large stores can put people off	5	
CS5				CW5			
CS6				CW6			
CS7				CW7			
CS8				CW8			
CS9				CW9			
CS10				CW10			

MARKET ATTRACTIVENESS

	CUSTOMER OPPORTUNITIES	I	GROUP		CUSTOMER THREATS	I	GROUP
CO1	Expand abroad	5		CT1	Any small slip in growth of sales hits profits hard	10	
CO2	Attract 'professional' customers	6		CT2	Could lose its independence	10	
CO3	Go into baby wear	4		CT3	Good economic times can lose customers to competition	5	
CO4	Use local relationships with MP's etc, to get new stores in the right place	5		CT4	Environmental legislation on packaging	5	
CO5				CT5			
CO6				CT6			
CO7				CT7			
CO8				CT8			
CO9				CT9			
CO10				CT10			

TITLE	DESCRIPTION	OWNER	DATE	VALUE	$

Fig. 7.3 Account planner for Ace Supermarkets.

TOP TEN SALES CAMPAIGNS							
SC1	TVdeserT	To sell this range into Ace		KL	dd/mm/yy	£50,000	A
SC2	Ace Fast	To break into this market with TVT products		DS	dd/mm/yy	£1 million/ year	R
SC3	Organic	To use a joint promotion to sell organic through some target stores		KL	dd/mm/yy	?	R
SC4							
SC5							
SC6							
SC7							
SC8							
SC9							
SC10							

OUR COMPETITIVENESS

OUR STRENGTHS		I	G	OUR WEAKNESSES		I	G
OS1	Efficient manufacturing still with flexibility	7	8	OW1	Poor brand awareness with consumers	10	7
OS2	Lowest 'returns' demonstrates quality	9	7	OW2	Lower level of contact than competition	6	1
OS3	Presence in Europe	5	1	OW3	No presence in consumer direct technology	8	4
OS4				OW4			
OS5				OW5			
OS6				OW6			
OS7				OW7			
OS8				OW8			
OS9				OW9			
OS10				OW10			

CUSTOMER ATTRACTIVENESS

OUR OPPORTUNITIES		I	GROUP	OUR THREATS		I	G
OO1	Introduce appropriate Ace people to European suppliers and customers	7	1	OT1	If we do not expand market share, they could dump us	10	7
OO2	Demonstrate our reputation with professionals	5	6	OT2	They retreat into their normal strong markets rather than seeking new types of consumer	7	5
OO3	Sell value by working on return on investment	7	2	OT3	If they are taken over we could lose out	9	8
OO4	Produce above average gross margin	9	8	OT4	They want a constant stream of new product	5	2
OO5				OT5			
OO6				OT6			
OO7				OT7			
OO8				OT8			
OO9				OT9			
OO10				OT10			

ACCOUNT READINESS GROUPS	S	SPIDER'S WEB

Fig. 7.3 (*continued*)

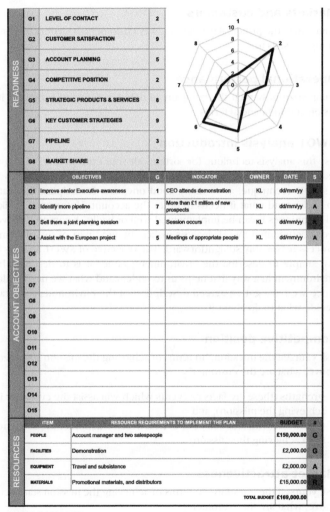

READINESS			
G1	LEVEL OF CONTACT	2	
G2	CUSTOMER SATISFACTION	9	
G3	ACCOUNT PLANNING	5	
G4	COMPETITIVE POSITION	2	
G5	STRATEGIC PRODUCTS & SERVICES	8	
G6	KEY CUSTOMER STRATEGIES	9	
G7	PIPELINE	3	
G8	MARKET SHARE	2	

ACCOUNT OBJECTIVES		OBJECTIVES	G	INDICATOR	OWNER	DATE	S
	O1	Improve senior Executive awareness	1	CEO attends demonstration	KL	dd/mm/yy	R
	O2	Identify more pipeline	7	More than £1 million of new prospects	KL	dd/mm/yy	A
	O3	Sell them a joint planning session	3	Session occurs	KL	dd/mm/yy	R
	O4	Assist with the European project	5	Meetings of appropriate people	KL	dd/mm/yy	A
	O5						
	O6						
	O7						
	O8						
	O9						
	O10						
	O11						
	O12						
	O13						
	O14						
	O15						

RESOURCES	ITEM	RESOURCE REQUIREMENTS TO IMPLEMENT THE PLAN	BUDGET	S
	PEOPLE	Account manager and two salespeople	£150,000.00	G
	FACILITIES	Demonstration	£2,000.00	G
	EQUIPMENT	Travel and subsistence	£2,000.00	A
	MATERIALS	Promotional materials, and distributors	£15,000.00	R
		TOTAL BUDGET	£169,000.00	

Acc Man figures.xls Page 3 of 3

Fig. 7.3 (*continued*)

Markets and customers

Summarize the principal markets and key customers that your customer company sells to.

Operational performance

Summarize how well the company is doing in terms of achieving its vision and in financial terms

SWOT analysis introduction

Use this analysis technique for sorting out your current level of knowledge into: strengths, weaknesses, opportunities, and threats. This is a simple technique, as so many good ones are, for helping the team to understand what it needs to do in the account. Unfortunately, like all techniques it can be implemented well or badly. A comprehensive, well-documented SWOT analysis makes the next part of the planning process reasonably straightforward. The objective of SWOT analysis is not simply to describe the environment; rather it is to describe the environment in a way that helps us to understand what we need to do. Once we have got an agreed description of the environment we can decide what to do about it.

Competitive position

Ask yourself the question "In terms of achieving the mission statement above, what are the customer's:

» strengths (these are facts or events which will assist the customer in achieving the mission); and
» weaknesses (these are facts or events which will hinder the customer from achieving the mission)."

Market attractiveness

Ask yourself the question "In terms of achieving the mission statement above, what are the customer's:

» opportunities (these are things that the customer could do which will improve the chances of achieving the mission);

» threats (these are facts or events which, if not addressed, will prevent the customer from achieving the mission); and

» I (I is the impact or relative importance of each SWOT statement)."

Group or sales campaign

In this column put the group from G1 to G8 where you believe the SWOT statement has an impact on you the selling team. For example, if you are selling technology and a customer weakness is that directors of the company are unaware of the potential of technology in a key area, then document that under G1 level of contact. This will in turn become an opportunity for the selling team that could turn into an action involving getting into touch with some senior people. You may fill in this column when you identify each SWOT statement, or do them all together when you have finished the customer SWOT.

If the customer SWOT statement does not fit into any of the groups, either the statement is irrelevant or it involves a definite selling opportunity for the supplying team. In this case identify which of the top 10 sales campaigns it refers to from SC1 to SC10.

Top 10 sales campaigns

» *Title*. This is an identifier for the campaign.
» *Description*. This is a short summary of your opportunity.
» *Owner*. This is the salesperson responsible for making the sale.
» *Date*. This is the expected order date.
» *Value*. This is the total sales value.
» *Status*. This is red, amber, or green, depending on how well the sales campaign is progressing. Red means that the customer is unlikely to go ahead with the project unless you persuade them to be more interested or that you are losing to the competition. Amber means that with some good hard selling work you may be able to win this but there is still quite a bit to do. Green means that unless circumstances change, you are likely to get this order at the date entered.

Our competitiveness

Use the same SWOT analysis techniques to describe the current state of your relationship with the key account.

Our strengths

Under this heading, document in short, simple but complete sentences the strengths that your company could exploit in striving to achieve the mission. An example of a badly stated strength is the bullet point "installed base." Ask yourselves the "So what?" question. We have a large installed base but so what? Better would be "Our installed base means that we have good technical and financial references in chemicals division." Use the "So what" question wherever the team is having trouble agreeing on a particular element of the SWOT.

Our weaknesses

Under this heading, document in short, simple but complete sentences the weaknesses that you will have to acknowledge or correct in the plan in striving to achieve the S-mission. A poor weakness statement would be "Competitive domination." This begs the question and does not help us to know what to do. Better would be "The competition has more control over the customer's strategy than we do." In this latter case the statement helps us to see what to do next.

Our opportunities

We must be more flexible in the opportunities section on the sentences discipline. In this case, bullet points may suffice. What is needed here is a creative brainstorm of all the things the team and the supplying company could do to try to reach the mission. Maximize your creativity, because this is where you employ the vision to change the world in your company's direction.

Threats

Threats have a dual function. On the one hand, they describe potential disruptions to the mission from external and often uncontrollable sources. On the other hand, it is often useful in the threats column to document what will happen if the weaknesses identified above are not addressed or if the mission statement is not achieved.

Just as in the weaknesses, it is poor practice to put the name of a major competitor simply as a threat. After all, if the threat is simply the name of a company, all you could do to remove the threat is buy them, shoot them, or join them. Better would be "If we fail to have more influence over the customer's strategy, a major competitor will be the decision maker in when we are asked to bid."

Notice how the SWOT analysis describes the environment; it does not decide what we are going to do. For example, that last threat could be a perfectly sensible way of running that part of the account in a highly productive way; it basically means if we are asked to bid we will win. We may decide therefore to deploy our resources elsewhere and live with that threat.

Account readiness

Against each of the account readiness groups put the status. This is red, amber, or green, depending on how well you are placed in this area. Red means that there is a major issue here, and that the team is very likely to set objectives and actions aimed at improving the position. Amber means that there is a problem here that will impact on your relationship and performance in this account if you do not set objectives and actions aimed at improving the situation. Green means that your current activities are getting a satisfactory result in this area, and that you are unlikely to require new specific actions.

The spider's web

From the values you have given to the weaknesses, opportunities, and threats, the spider's web shows in diagrammatical form where your account priorities should go.

Account management objectives

You now have a good analysis of your strengths and weaknesses. It is time to prioritize these and as a team set your aspirations for the account. You will use the power of well-composed team objectives to change the world. The attributes of a well-worded objective or goal are:

» stretching – the goal has to be difficult enough to be worth doing;
» measurable – you must set a measure that defines successful performance;
» achievable – there is no point in trying to achieve the impossible;
» related to the customer – make sure the goal shows what is in it for the customer as well as for you; and
» time targeted – put a time measure on the goal.

Account management goals reflect the longer term relationship between the two companies and deal with the quality of that relationship as well as with other measures that are easier to quantify.

The SMART template is more difficult to apply to account management goals. The team will have to allow more flexibility without compromising the aim of a goal, which is to make it possible for the team to monitor its success in implementing the plan.

Taking the spider's web, look first at the priority areas, which are the points on which it scores lowest.

» *Objectives*. This is a team objective aimed at improving the position in the account.
» *G*. This is the group, G1 to G8, that the objective aims to improve. There may be more than one objective for a particular group.
» *Indicator*. What is the measure that you will use to check that you have achieved this objective?
» *Owner*. This is the team member accountable for the achievement of this objective.
» *Date*. This is the date by which the team should achieve the objective.
» *Status*. Red, amber, or green shows how likely the team is to achieve the objective by the due date.
» *Open items*. For each objective, define the actions you will need to undertake to achieve the goal and document them in the open item part of the tool.
» *Resources*. Finally, identify what special resources and budget are going to be required for this account. Think about what is to be achieved, and then quantify the resources in terms of: people, facilities, equipment, and materials.

INSIGHTS

At various stages in the production of an account plan the team members should validate their work with the customer. This strengthens the plan and the customer will add value even in places where they are not yet persuaded of your plans for the future. The more you involve the customer in the account planning cycle, the more likely you will be to implement the plan successfully.

Key Concepts
and Thinkers in
Account Management

The main part of this chapter describes the key words and concepts
used in selling and account management:

» words of wisdom on team planning and consultative selling; and
» a glossary of terms.

There is a lot of sales jargon about, and it is important that account teams, particularly international ones, use terms to mean the same thing. The bulk of this chapter, therefore, is a glossary of those terms.

But first some thinkers. Two people who have had a lot of influence in using team business processes to make good decisions for the future are Charles H. Kepner and Benjamin B. Tregoe. Many consultants in the account management line have learnt from another thinker, Mack Hanan, who took solution selling and account planning to its logical conclusion with his book *Consultative Selling*.[1]

KEY THINKERS

Charles H. Kepner and Benjamin B. Tregoe

These founders of the training and consultancy company that bears their name based their process consultancy on research into what makes some individuals and teams more effective than others. An outline of their findings is that more effective managers used a "process" approach, and that the process they used varied from situation to situation. They found that people were unwilling to get into discussion on an important decision if there was no systematic procedure to follow. They argued that it was difficult for people to discuss plans because of the feelings that the participants had that important aspects of the plan would be missed out, or that some options outside the ones being promoted by members of the team were bound to exist and would be missed by the group. This leads to what Kepner and Tregoe called making decisions through the "shoving process," in which the person with the most power is bound to prevail.

But if people are given a common approach to decision making, the teamwork improves and the decision arrived at depends on the activities and thinking processes of the whole team. That is, it is the systematic process that stops decision making being a one-person activity and allows brainstorming techniques to offer more creative options and reach a better decision. They said:

"Decision Analysis is a systematic procedure based on the thinking pattern we use when making choices. Its techniques represent expansion and refinement of the elements in this thinking pattern:

We appreciate the fact that a choice must be made

We consider the specific factors that must be satisfied if the choice is to succeed

We decide what kind of action will best satisfy these factors

We consider what risks may be attached to our final choice of action that could jeopardize its safety and success."

Kepner and Tregoe[2]

Transferred to the multitude of decisions made in an account plan, these findings have fueled attempts to systemize the account planning process.

Consultative selling

Many salespeople assure their prospects and customers that if they buy from them they will be investing in not just a supplier of goods and services, but also a partner for their operation. Many assure, but few actually deliver on this promise. Indeed, if you probe them, few can actually define what a partnership between a customer and a supplier is.

Mack Hanan's book *Consultative Selling* gives as good a definition of the processes involved in becoming your customer's partner as you can get. His starting point is this:

"Consultative selling is profit improvement selling. It is selling to high-level customer decision makers who are concerned with profit – indeed who are responsible for it, measured by it, evaluated by it and accountable for it."

The process involves analyzing trends in the customer's product/markets, researching the customer's business, developing customer strategies for growth, and finally recommending actions that the customer should take to improve their profits. If you do this, Hanan maintains, you will be pretty much immune from competitors because you are offering a much more valuable kind of service. In fact the supplier is more or less going through the same process as the customer.

The consultative selling process includes becoming involved in the customer's evaluation of your proposition from a return on investment perspective. Hanan says:

"An opportunity window opens for [the salesperson] when the following conditions are met:
  1 The dollar value of the profits from your solution exceed the dollar value of the customer's problem.
  2 The dollar value of the profits from your solution exceed the dollar value of the costs of your solution.
  3 The dollar value of the profits from your solution exceed the dollar value of the profits from competitive solutions."

In order to know this, the salesperson has to be privy to the customer's process of investment appraisal and purchasing, with an emphasis on the financial side, and to be able to assist the customer to estimate the benefits of the solution. It is not easy to get into that position with a customer; it requires a high level of contact and an even higher level of confidence in the account manager and their integrity. But it can be done as long as the salespeople can ask the right questions and use their, or their own finance people's, knowledge to assist the customer in this way.

As long as the average salesperson still imagines that his or her greatest skill is to describe the features of their products and services in sometimes insufferable detail, professional account managers who join in the debate about the way ahead for their customers with the senior managers they deal with have an immense competitive edge.

GLOSSARY OF TERMS

Account goals – Specific objectives concerned with improving a supplier's long-term relationship with a customer.

Account management – The ongoing strategic direction of major clients' business.

Account planning – The process of producing a team plan of action for an account.

Benefits – Those things that the service does for or means to buyers, rather than the factual descriptions of it (which are the features).

Buying signals – Signs that the buyer is at a stage of understanding and acceptance that permits closing to be tried.

Call frequency – The number of times in a year a customer is scheduled to receive regular calls; sometimes used to categorize customers and describe their relative importance.

Call plan – The statement of work to be done with customers arranged with productivity and effectiveness in mind.

Client records – The basis of information, from contact details to buying record, that can be consulted in planning the next action with existing and past clients.

Closing – Action taken to gain a commitment to buy or proceed onwards towards the point where this can logically occur.

Cold calling – Approaches to potential customers by any method (face to face or telephone, say) who are "cold" – have expressed no prior interest of any sort.

Competitor intelligence – The information collected about competitive products and services and their suppliers that may specifically be used to improve the approach taken on a call.

Consultative selling – Assisting the customer to improve profitability by buying products and services.

Cost justification – The part of the sales argument that deals directly with price, relating it to results or benefits and describing value for money.

Cross-selling – The technique of selling another product related to the first, like selling a tie to someone who has just bought a shirt, ensuring that a range of different services are bought from a client who starts by buying only one.

Cross-culture – Dealing with different geographical cultures in the same account.

Curbside conference – The post-call "post-mortem" and development session held when a sales manager is accompanying salespeople in the field (which may often take place in the car – hence the name).

Ego drive/empathy – Mayer and Goldberg's terms for, respectively, the internal motivational drive that makes the good salesperson *want* to succeed, and the ability to see things from other people's (customers') point of view – and, importantly, being seen to do so.

Farmers – Salespeople working on existing customers to improve the penetration of their products and services.

Features – The factual things to be described about a service (see Benefits).

Field training – Training or development activity away from any formal setting, undertaken out and about on territory.

Gatekeeper – Someone who through their position can facilitate or deny access to a buyer (e.g. a secretary).

Groundrules – The essential rules that govern a team planning process.

Handling objections – The stage of sales presentations which is most highly interactive and where specific queries (or challenges) posed by potential buyers must be addressed to keep the positive side of the case in the majority.

Hunters – Salespeople who specialize in finding new customers.

Influencers – People who, while not having exclusive authority to buy, influence the buyer, through, say, their recommendation.

Key/major/national accounts – A variety of names are used here. First, measures vary as to what a major customer is; simplistically it is only what an individual organization finds significant. A second significant factor is the lead time involved. In industries selling, say, capital equipment it may take many months from first meeting to contract and there is an overlap here with "major sales."

Need identification – The process of asking questions to discover what – exactly what – clients want (and why) as a basis for deciding how to pitch the sales presentation.

Negotiation – A different, though closely allied, skill to selling and very important in some kinds of business (*note:* there is another *Express-Exec* volume Negotiating, which can provide a useful reference).

On-the-job training – Field training and development activity, often starting with joint calls with a manager.

Partnership – The mutual relationship between a key account and a supplier. Often defined as existing when the two organizations are involved in each other's planning process.

Petal system – A practical way of organizing journeys to minimize time and mileage and thus help maximize productivity.

Pie system - A structured way of managing the spread of customers and prospects around a sales territory.

Pitch - A formal presentation which is part of the sales process; may be general or in response to a specific brief.

Proposal - Normally implies a written document, one including the price but more than a quotation - it spells out the case and most often reflects a clear brief which has been given or established.

Prospecting - The search for new contacts who may be potential clients; encompasses everything from cold calling to desk research to identify names.

Qualifying prospects - Research or action to produce information to demonstrate that cold prospects are "warm."

Sales aids - Anything used during the sales conversation to enhance what is said; may be items, information (say a graph), or even other people.

Sales audit - An, occasional, systematic review of all aspects of the sales activity and its management to identify areas needing improvement, or working well and needing extension; a process that recognizes the inherent dynamic nature of sales.

Sales productivity - The sales equivalent of productivity in an area, the focus here is on efficiencies that maximize the amount of time spent with customers (rather than traveling, writing reports, etc.): it focuses on ratios and touches on anything that increases sales success, however measured.

Solution selling - The activities involved in demonstrating how your products and services will solve a customer's problem and improve their key financial measures.

SPIN - Although this is a registered trademark, it is heard used generically - spin - to describe a customer-focused and questioning-based approach to identifying needs and selling appropriately in light of this knowledge.

Standards - Preset targets (absolute, moving, or diagnostic standards are all used) used to direct sales activity and to set objectives.

SWOT analysis - Environmental analysis at the beginning of a planning process to identify the strengths, weaknesses, opportunities, and threats in the customer's or supplier's current situation.

Team selling – Selling in partnership with others together in the same meeting; might be colleagues or collaborators.

Territory – The area covered by an individual salesperson. It is usually, but not always, geographic.

Tools – Templates used to use and share business processes.

NOTES

1 Hanan, Mack (1985) *Consultative Selling*. Amacom, New York.

2 Kepner, Charles H. and Tregoe, Benjamin B. (1997) *The New Rational Manager*. Princeton Research Press, Princeton, NJ.

Resources for Account Management

This chapter refers to the basic resource document of an account plan:

» using the annual report of a key account as a starting point; and
» a free Website with valuable management insights.

THE COMPANY'S ANNUAL REPORT

Account managers sometimes underestimate the usefulness of the published annual report of the account they manage. Many experienced account managers, however, justifiably use a quote from the customer's annual report to start off any presentation that they make. It must, after all, introduce the topic of the presentation in the light of the company's strategies or issues – not a bad starting point for a team trying to impress managers that the propositions they make to the key account have strategic fit.

> "Customers   How do they see us?
>   Internal   What must we excel at?
>   Financial   How do shareholders see us?
>   Innovation   How can we continue to learn, improve and add value?"
>
> *Kaplan and Norton describing the balanced scorecard*[1]

Used well, the annual report gives us answers to the Kaplan–Norton questions above. Some people, comfortable with the financial pages, tend to ignore the rest of the report. They argue that the other text reports are mere advertisements for the company and the brilliance of its directors, while the financial pages are regulated in such a way that they represent the truth about the company. Unfortunately neither of these statements is entirely true. Companies do use "creative accounting" that sticks to the letter of the law, but paints a picture that misleads rather than guides the reader. On the other hand, those who are less comfortable with the financial side try to make do with the other parts of the report to try to understand the enterprise. But it is of little use to understand the director's view of the forward strategy of the company if you cannot check whether the financial situation the company is in will allow them to implement it. A company, for example, talking about growth by acquisition is less likely to succeed if financially they are already in a lot of debt. Shareholders in the acquisitive dot.com companies suffered badly from this if they did not check just how huge the debt problem for the acquirer was becoming.

The contents of an annual report

The chairman and directors of a company use the annual report as an advertising document as well as the means to satisfy legal reporting requirements. They are unlikely to open with a sentence such as "We made a lot of mistakes this year and have to own up to a performance far below the potential of the business." Scything through the propaganda is possible, however, for one very important reason. Unless engaged in actual fraud, luckily a remote possibility, they are bound to stick to the truth, albeit in its most acceptable form. The "spin" is there but in most cases a little detective work will reveal what the account team needs to know.

Remember also that probably the key performance measure of a chairman is his or her ability to deliver to their business plan. This means announcing what the future of the business should be and then achieving it. This achievement of expectations is a principal concern of shareholders who have set their own strategy in deciding on the type and qualities of the company they want to buy. The shareholders acknowledge, of course, that there is a risk that not all of these expectations will be delivered.

It is for this reason that you may from time to time hear of profit warnings emanating from your key account. A chairman who realizes that the company is not going to be as profitable as he or she led the shareholders and analysts to expect will tell them the moment the information is clear and the likelihood of underperforming is high. When this happens, God help the account manager who ignores it. It will have an impact on them soon enough.

This expectation is particularly important in the case of the dividend which shareholders have been led to expect from previous performance or from a statement of dividend strategy from the board. In order to meet expectations on dividend, the company has to deliver to expectations on profit and cash. It needs the profit to cover the costs of the dividend and the requirement for the future of the business, and it needs the cash to actually pay out the dividend amounts. Shareholders will not take it in any other form, and a bouncing dividend check is highly unpopular! These drivers impact on the company's strategy and therefore on the strategy of the account team selling to it.

Mission statement

Many companies put their statement of intent, or their mission statement, on the front cover or in a key position on the first page. It is a
key vision and strategy statement. They tend now to be getting shorter
and more useful. The account manager should study it and use it to
test the validity of what comes later. Every strategy statement and plan
for the future should echo this mission statement, both in the annual
report and, more importantly, in the account plan.

Financial highlights

The inside cover and first page normally contain the company's view of
their financial performance last year compared to the year before. This
is interesting but carefully picked. If you want a more independent and
consistent way of looking at the financial progress of a company, you
will need to use your own tool to make your own interpretation.

The chairman's statement

This is always a key description of the intentions of the company. It is
impossible to predict what will be in any particular statement except to
say that the chairman will pick out the critical issues in the recent past
and in the future. Often these critical issues are what account managers
have to form an opinion on. They may well reveal opportunities for the
selling team; threats that the current team plan will not work.

The headings below are almost always covered in the chairman's
statement:

» last year's financial performance;
» dividends;
» the way ahead; and
» structure and people.

Last year's financial performance

As part of the historical performance, the chairman will normally
comment on the main trading issues of the past year. He or she will put
them into the context of the economic situation in the main countries
where the company does business and mention other factors outside

the board's control which have had an impact, normally a negative impact, on the past year's performance.

Dividends

In almost all cases, you will see a statement in the chairman's report that conveys the increase or decrease in dividend proposed this year, and which can be read as the board's strategy on dividend in the future.

The way ahead

The chairman here picks out the vital issues involved in the next period of trading. Look carefully at this as you are going to have to feel confident that the issue is in reality what will drive performance and that your plan for the account fits in.

In most reports the "prospects" section will reveal what the company believes is its main competitive advantage. If the account manager can demonstrate that the products and services they are selling assist this differentiation, all the better.

Structure and people

At this stage in the statement it is very likely that chairman will comment on the company structure and the quality of the company's people – vital background information for the account team.

Reports of the chief executive and directors

This report will contain a number of matters required by law. It may also include statements from the directors on the position of the company in a number of areas.

Principal activities

This is, as it suggests, a short statement of the principal businesses which the group is in.

Research and development

This outlines the R&D that is being undertaken by the company. Later in the notes to the accounts you will see the actual amount of money spent.

Directors

At this point there is a series of items of information about the directors, their resigning by rotation, and their interest in the company's shares. In many reports, rather than having the interests of the directors stated at this point, there is a reference to where this information can be found further into the report. This may very well help to determine where real power lies in the buying organization.

Conclusion to the report of the directors

The company secretary, who generally has some legal training, signs the report. In larger companies the company secretary may very well be the most senior legal officer in the company, and an important source of information on the legal terms and conditions the company operates with its suppliers.

Review of operations

This is an important statement from which the account team can derive the company's strategy. The detection of the overall strategy should not be too difficult. After all, the board of a company is responsible for analyzing possible future plans, deciding on the appropriate strategy, and then communicating this to all the people who will be involved in its execution. Those involved in the execution are staff at all levels and in all functions. It is necessary that a consistent pyramid of plans ensures that what is happening on the shop floor and at the point of sale and delivery fits in with the plans of the directors. It is equally important that the plans of its key suppliers also fit in. This communication is very difficult to get right, and its failure is obvious to staff and customers alike.

The account manager, however, needs a simple technique for detecting and documenting the board's strategy. The team should do this by means of the company activity matrix. The review of operations will contain, in some form, statements of the company's products and markets' segmentation and we should be able to reproduce this in a simple matrix (see Fig. 9.1). The harder the exercise is to do, the less well is the board explaining itself, probably to shareholders and staff alike.

	Market 1	Market 2	Market 3	Market 4	Market 5	Market 6	Market 7	Market 8
Product 1								
Product 2								
Product 3								
Product 4								
Product 5								

Fig. 9.1 The activity matrix.

A USEFUL FREE WEBSITE

www.managementlearning.com – This Website carries a lot of insights and ideas for many different types of manager. Use it for understanding your role better, and also to understand how managers in your key account use best practice to carry out their functions.

NOTES

1 Kaplan, Robert S. and Norton, David P. (1996) *The Balanced Scorecard*. Harvard Business Press, Cambridge, Mass.

Ten Steps to Implementing Account Management

Account management techniques are one thing. Putting them into practice to produce an account plan is another. Here are the 10 steps necessary to do that.

1 Agree the customer-mission.
2 The customer-SWOT.
3 Agree the supplier-mission.
4 The supplier-SWOT.
5 Cross-check the customer-SWOT to the supplier-SWOT.
6 Agree the account team's critical success factors.
7 Produce the control matrix.
8 Agree the spider's web.
9 Set the account management goals for the account.
10 Set the strategy for achieving the goals, and creating action plans.

Let us assume that you have prepared a room, got the flipcharts ready, and assembled the appropriate people to build the plan. With or without a facilitator, go through the creative planning process.

1. AGREE THE CUSTOMER-MISSION

Normally the driving force of an account team's plan will be a statement of a customer aim – in the planning process. This is the customer mission statement, or C-mission. This can be huge or small, a corporate aim or a focused project. Be careful not to bite off more than the team can chew. It is better to do a high-quality plan on a single division, rather than a less well-informed plan on the whole organization.

Take a large publishing group incorporating many companies. Its strategy is to divide the group into three global markets aimed at information, education, and entertainment. An account team which has a strong presence in, say, the publishing part of the company might very well limit the account plan to the information companies. Still plenty of scope, but focused on that part of the business the team knows best.

If the team is experienced and has strength in all parts of the account it is planning, then it will start with the vision of the company in question. Vision statements tend to follow a pattern. They start from an aspiration to a continuing achievement "To be ...." This is followed by a superlative, for example "the best" or "the most successful." There follows a description of the business or business operation and a geographic area. If the planning team chooses such a broad mission as the driver of the planning session, it will take a very comprehensive view of the account.

It is important to get the C-mission right as it kicks off the direction and scope of the planning session. But the team must not become inflexible. If during the next stage of the process it finds the mission statement to be slightly or wholly wrong, it does not normally take much effort to change it and correct all the subsequent work.

It is likely that the account manager will have the C-mission prepared before the start of the planning session. Once the whole team has agreed the message and content of the C-mission, it is stuck on the wall in a prominent position and remains throughout the session, a helpful reminder of the scope of the session.

2. THE C-SWOT

Onto a flipchart write the following words and headings:

> "In terms of achieving that mission the customer has the following:
> STRENGTHS
> WEAKNESSES
> OPPORTUNITIES
> THREATS"

Strengths

Under this heading, document in short, simple but complete sentences the strengths the customer could exploit in striving to achieve the mission. Some teams like to start from a series of bullet points and then expand them into sentences. As we will see, however, it is much easier to proceed to the next part of the process if the team eventually obeys the discipline of short, simple but complete sentences.

It is very useful to distinguish the SWOT analysis by color. Use blue for strengths, red for weaknesses, green for opportunities, and black for threats. As the team completes each chart, pin or stick it to the wall. It is then a relatively simple task to locate SWOT statements later in the process.

Weaknesses

Under this heading, document in short, simple but complete sentences the weaknesses the customer will have to acknowledge or correct in their plan in striving to achieve the mission. Spend enough time on the weaknesses section as it will probably contain the germs of your, the selling company's, opportunities. Having said that, keep the SWOT broad and focused on the customer, not on the products and services that you sell.

Opportunities

You must be more flexible in the opportunities section on the sentences discipline. In this case, bullet points may suffice. What is needed here is a creative brainstorm of all the things the customer could do to try to reach the C-mission. Let it all hang out and do not reject anything at this stage. You will have an opportunity subsequently to check the feasibility of the ideas with the customer.

At this point the team must make an important check to ensure that there is consistency between the weaknesses and opportunities part of the SWOT analysis. Before moving on to the threats part of the analysis process, get the team to check through the weaknesses section of the SWOT. Has the team identified improvements or changes the customer could make to address each and every one of the weaknesses? This ensures the comprehensiveness of the opportunities section.

Threats

Threats have a dual function. On the one hand, they describe potential disruptions to the customer mission from external and often uncontrollable sources. On the other hand, it is often useful in the threats column to document what will happen if the weaknesses identified above are not addressed or if the mission statement is not achieved.

The C-SWOT stretches the account team's customer knowledge to its limits and frequently produces a "We do not know" list which fits into the supplier weaknesses part of the SWOT analysis. The stronger the C-SWOT the more customer oriented is the resulting plan. Of course, the ultimate in C-SWOT is to persuade the customer to go through the process with the supplier account team. This joint planning is an aiming point for most account teams.

In any case, the account manager should take the C-SWOT to the customer. Most executives are very impressed by the fact that the selling team have gone to such lengths in trying to provide solutions. Psychologically they are in a position where they will probably want to agree with some of the statements and correct or modify others.

Number each of the strengths, weaknesses, opportunities, and threats individually when it is agreed that the C-SWOT has been completed for reference purposes.

3. AGREE THE SUPPLIER-MISSION

The S-mission is an outline aim of what the supplier wants to achieve in the part of the customer's business described in the C-mission and C-SWOT. As with the C-mission, the S-mission can be very broad or more focused. If, however, the focus is more or less on one sales objective, the team should check whether key account planning is the appropriate process, or whether it would be better off doing a campaign plan. It is likely that the account manager will bring the S-mission with him or her, in which case it only requires the team to buy into it before the supplier part of the environmental analysis starts in earnest.

If it is helpful, many teams start the whole planning session with the S-mission. They find that they need that focus before starting on the customer analysis. Be flexible and find the way that suits your team.

4. THE S-SWOT

Onto a flipchart write the following words and headings:

"In terms of achieving that mission we have the following:
STRENGTHS
WEAKNESSES
OPPORTUNITIES
THREATS"

Strengths

Under this heading, document in short, simple but complete sentences the strengths your company could exploit in striving to achieve the S-mission. An example of a badly stated strength is the bullet point "installed base." Ask yourselves the "So what?" question. We have a large installed base but so what? Use the "So what" question wherever the team is having trouble agreeing on a particular element of the SWOT.

Weaknesses

Under this heading, document in short, simple but complete sentences the weaknesses you will have to acknowledge or correct in the plan in striving to achieve the S-mission. A poor weakness statement would be "IBM domination." This begs the question and does not help us to know what to do. Better would be "IBM has more control over the customer's IT strategy than we do.'' In this latter case the statement helps us to see what to do next.

Opportunities

We must be more flexible in the opportunities section on the sentences discipline. In this case, bullet points may suffice. What is needed here is a creative brainstorm of all the things the team and the supplying company could do to try to reach the S-mission. Maximize your creativity, because this is where you employ the vision to change the world in your company's direction.

Threats

Threats have a dual function. On the one hand, they describe potential disruptions to the S-mission from external and often uncontrollable sources. On the other hand, it is often useful in the threats column to document what will happen if the weaknesses identified above are not addressed or if the mission statement is not achieved. Just as in the weaknesses, it is poor practice to put the name of a major competitor as a threat. After all, if the threat is simply the name of a company, all you could do to remove the threat is buy them, shoot them, or join them.

Notice how the SWOT analysis describes the environment, it does not decide what we are going to do. That comes later. The S-SWOT and its quality are the key to the success of the plan.

5. CROSS-CHECK THE C-SWOT TO THE S-SWOT

You will notice that in composing the S-SWOT the team makes frequent reference to the C-SWOT. At this point it is worth doing a specific check. The weaknesses section of the C-SWOT describes the key issues the customer has to do something about to achieve their aim. We must ensure that there is a corresponding supplier opportunity for as many of these weaknesses as possible. Often they will not be opportunities to do with our normal products and services. They may, for example, be opportunities to help the customer plan or review some business process or policy. If there is no connection between the customer's weaknesses and the supplier's opportunities, you have a major problem, since we are not assisting the customer to address their key issues.

That check being complete, we only need the S-SWOT as the reference point for goal setting. The C-SWOT can be ignored as all the key customer issues have come through to the plan via the S-opportunities.

Summary of the position at the end of the SWOT analysis

All round the room is a logical progression from the C-mission through the C-SWOT, S-mission, and S-SWOT on flipcharts. We now need to decide what to do and we need to control the connection between the SWOT analysis and our activities. The team now needs a bridging mechanism which will act as a connector between the SWOT analysis and goal setting. Without this simple device it is very difficult to get a good link, and to know where to start.

A bit like eating an elephant (start by eating the tail), this bridge and the spider's web technique help the team to move efficiently into the next phase of the plan.

6. AGREE THE ACCOUNT TEAM'S CRITICAL SUCCESS FACTORS

Experience has helped to define some general critical success factors (csf) for professional account management (see Table 10.1). Starting from these the team should decide which of them is 100% relevant to its situation, which need modification, and which, if any, need to be scrapped or replaced by another.

Before moving on to the next step, the team should revise its S-SWOT in the light of the account management critical success factors. Table 10.2 contains a checklist of questions in each of the areas.

7. PRODUCE THE CONTROL MATRIX

The situation now is that the team has generated a SWOT analysis encompassing all the key issues of its environment. It will be quite long – maybe 15 strengths, 30 weaknesses, 15 opportunities, and 5

Table 10.1 General critical success factors for professional account management.

Account management csf	Short definition
Level of contact	Assesses how well the team is placed to get to all the key people in the account
Customer satisfaction/supplier contribution	Measures how well we have kept our promises and provided customer satisfaction. Also measures whether or not the selling team has agreed with the customer the contribution it and its products and services have made to the customer's business
Account planning	Looks at the state and quality of the team's plans – both account plans and campaign plans
Competitive position	Looks at the two issues of protecting current market share and increasing it
Strategic applications, products, and services	Assesses the fit between the customer's way ahead and the products and services of the supplying company in terms of strategic importance and leverage
Key customer strategies	In any key account there are some policy or strategy statements that have a major impact on the selling team's ability to do business. The team agrees at this stage how positive or negative these strategies are for its continuing success
Pipeline	Measures the team's sales pipeline to ensure that there are enough opportunities for making sales in the short to medium term to achieve its business targets
Market share	Looks at the overall trend of market share

threats. Before turning to goal setting, the team needs to group the SWOT analysis into manageable parts. You need to allocate each strength, weakness, opportunity, and threat to an account management goal area. The method is this.

Table 10.2   Checklist of questions.

Account management csf	Checklist of sub-questions
Level of contact	Do you have regular contacts at all levels? Senior management? High level within your product users? High and wide at technical level? Where necessary in central purchasing?
Customer satisfaction/supplier contribution	Do you have an agreed measure of customer satisfaction with the customer? Do you deliver what you promised on time and within budget? Does the product give the expected performance? Is there a method of calculating the return on investment of previous projects you have supplied?
Account planning	Does the account plan have the agreement of all the team members worldwide? Does the pyramid of plans which links the main account plan to sub-account plans exist? Do you have campaign plans in place for all major sales campaigns? Have all the necessary resources agreed to make their contribution to all your plans?
Competitive position	Are you aware of the strengths and weaknesses of the main competitors you are facing? Are you aware of your company's strengths and weaknesses in relation to the competition? How vulnerable is your installed base to competitive attack? Are you seen as price competitive and value for money?

(continued overleaf)

Table 10.2 (*continued*)

Account management csf	Checklist of sub-questions
Strategic applications, products, and services	Has previous work you have done got you into a position where what you supply is strategically important to the customer?
	Can you leverage other sales from previous ones?
	Do you currently have a proposal to make which will have this strategic impact?
Key customer strategies	Is the team thoroughly aware of your company's product strategy and can they articulate it to your customer?
	Is there a good connection between your plan and your customer's overall strategy?
	Can you see the connection between your plan and some customer critical success factors?
Pipeline	Do you know early enough in the customer's buying process when bids are being invited?
	Do you have enough prospects in the pipeline to ensure that you will make target even if your biggest project fails to close?
	Have you got a plan for regular prospecting for new opportunities?
Market share	Do you have an acceptable measure of what your market share is?
	Do your campaigns deliver market share in line with your company's goals?

1 Number the SWOT analysis so that each strength, weakness, opportunity, and threat is identifiable.
2 Now draw the control matrix as in Table 10.3.
3. Being careful to obey the color code, ask the team to group the SWOT analysis. In about three-quarters of an hour the team will identify each weakness, opportunity, and threat with one goal area.

Table 10.3 Control matrix chart.

Goal area	Remove weakness	Exploit opportunity	Avoid threat	Use strength
Level of contact	8, 9, 23	3, 4, 8, 9, 14	1, 3, 4	1, 3, 4, 6, 8, 12
Customer satisfaction/supplier contribution	2, 3, 7, 15, 16	1, 2, 5	2, 6, 10	2, 4, 6, 8, 10
Account planning	21, 22	6, 10, 11, 12	7, 8, 11	1, 3, 4, 7, 8, 9
Competitive position	4, 5, 6, 10, 11, 12	7, 13	5, 9	2, 8, 9, 12
Strategic applications, products, and services	1, 17, 24	16		2, 7, 8, 9, 11
Key customer strategies	13, 14, 18, 19, 20	15	12, 13	13, 14
Pipeline	25, 27	19, 22	14, 15	9, 11, 13
Market share	26, 28, 29	17, 18, 20, 21	16	2, 8, 12, 13

Obey this rule if possible – "Only allocate a weakness, opportunity, or threat to one goal area." As we will see at goal setting and action planning, we are getting near allocating responsibility for the achievement of progress in the plan to individuals. Each W, O, and T will probably represent a milestone in the activity plan. It is important, therefore, that no action falls between two people's responsibility. Thus the rule.

When it comes to strengths, we may of course put each strength into as many goal areas as possible. At action planning time, the team will use the strengths as pointers to what they can exploit to eliminate weaknesses.

8. AGREE THE SPIDER'S WEB

The team is now in position, before moving to goal setting, to use the spider's web technique to assess our overall position in the account. The spider's web derives from the agreed critical success factors of good account management. The assessment consists of the team marking itself subjectively out of 10 in each of the 8 areas: 0 out of 10 – very bad position; 10 out of 10 – could not be better.

In the example below it is assumed that the team is looking at the key account as a whole and that the selling company is a systems integrator selling a whole variety of hardware, software, and consultancy products. It is of course possible, and desirable, to make the assessment at many, if not all, levels inside a large account. In this case each sub-accountee will maintain this diagrammatic representation of the health of his or her part of the account.

Level of contact

A score of 10/10 would mean that the supplier has regular business meetings at top level and very widely in the account. The test is height and width. A good score would reflect talking at top level, at high level within the user community, and at top level in the IT organization. A poor performance would reflect, for example, the only contact being in the IT department of a subsidiary where the supplier has done business. Notice the contact must be at business meetings. If we only meet the chief executive once a year at the ballet, that fails the test of top-level contact.

This is a very key test because if the team scores low here then other goal areas are made impossible to do well, e.g. account planning.

Customer satisfaction/supplier contribution

As with many of these goal areas this test breaks into two sets of marks out of 5 rather than one out of 10.

Customer satisfaction

This reflects the normal supplier measure of customer satisfaction. Did we deliver what we promised on time and within budget? Does the hardware and software give the expected up-time? When there are problems, are they fixed quickly? Are we supporting the sites properly?

A customer satisfaction survey gives good clues for this test, but it should be remembered that such a survey reflects what the customer believes is good customer satisfaction. What we really need here is a test of what the customer believes and agrees with us is a satisfactory performance. Top-rate account managers will negotiate with the customer a level of satisfaction which the customer finds acceptable, and which the account manager can sell internally to those parts of the supplier organization which are involved in delivering the promises.

Supplier contribution

This measures the agreed impact that projects previously implemented by the supplier have had on the customer's business. The keys are reductions in costs, avoidance of costs, improved decision making, and control. In other words, return on investment (RoI). We will score highly here if we are involved in the cost/benefit analysis which the customer does before investing, and also involved in measuring the impact of projects once implemented – the audit function. We will score low if we are unaware of the processes the customer has in place for estimating RoI or if the customer never does any *post-hoc* cost justification.

This is an area where teams can achieve competitive edge if they are the only supplier that tries to help the customer to do this. There is no better opening to a presentation of a new project than to open with the positive business impact of previous projects.

Account planning

What is the state of our account planning? Do we have a plan which meets the rules of a top quality plan?

A top quality plan:

» is approved by everyone involved;
» reflects the customer's own business plan;
» has predicted results which are stretching but credible;
» includes identified and committed resources from the supplier and the customer;
» is backed by a huge "knowledge database" of the customer's environment;
» conforms to a standard format where one is in place;
» includes clearly identified key dependencies;
» contains measurable milestones for all objectives;
» is regularly updated to reflect change and team achievements;
» incorporates ideas derived "top down" and "bottom up;" and
» stands alone as a communication of an account team's intentions.

A high score here will mean that the customer has been involved at some point in the planning process and that those parts of the plan which they need to agree are complete and agreed. Notice that it is impossible for the plan to reflect the customer's own business plan if the team scores poorly on level of contact.

The team also scores itself for the state of its campaign plans for crucial sales situations.

Competitive position

This breaks into two parts.

» How vulnerable is our installed base? Is any of it under competitive attack? Would it be relatively easy for the customer to remove our presence and replace our products and services with competitive ones?
» Looking into the future, do our strengths against the competition give us a fighting chance of breaking into competitive areas? The key here is to understand what the strengths and weaknesses are of our product portfolio and the competition's.

Strategic applications, products, and services

This looks at the leverage that can come from the installed base or from an identified potential sale. Has what we have already sold given us significant competitive edge for future projects and made a strategic contribution to the customer's business? Score highly if so and also if such a strategic application, product, or service is being actively considered by the customer for future implementation. If such a project is being considered, we may need a heavier weight of resources in relation to the supplier short-term benefit.

Key customer strategies

A two-part question:

» Does the customer strategy broadly reflect the supplier's approach? Is it easy to see a link between the supplier's product and services strategy and the main customer policies that have a major impact on our ability to make sales?

The team must first reach a decision as to which customer strategies are involved. In the computer industry, the key strategy will be the one (or ones) that concern IT and telecommunications.

Keep your thinking wide. This is not just a question of, for example, a technology strategy; it is also concerned with the customer's strategic requirements, management strategy, and business processes.

» Are we, the supplying team, involved in the process the customer uses to review these strategies? A systems integrator scores highly here if it is continuously asked for opinions and for input to strategic IT planning. The same team scores low if a competitor holds that position.

Pipeline

In order to improve market share we need to have identified where and when the customer is going to invest. This investment program shows the rate of growth of the market and allows us to forecast what our short- and medium-term revenues are going to be.

A full *pipeline* of potential business covering what we need to sell in order to meet our market-share aspiration many times over gives a high score here. A high score should also mean that the team is less vulnerable to a delay in one large project by the customer throwing the whole plan into disarray. We also need to know early in the customer's buying process when bids are being invited. A good score in this reflects the fact that the systems integrator is involved heavily in the applications strategy.

The supplier is probably also helping the customer in project evaluation before the customer gets to the nitty-gritty of choosing hardware and software. A poor score could be caused by the fact that we only know about a bid when the specification lands on our desk, or where the customer makes a lot of hardware and software investments without our participation or even knowledge.

Market share

In the end, this is what it is all about. Using a sensible measure, is our market share significant, and is it rising? The litmus test of successful

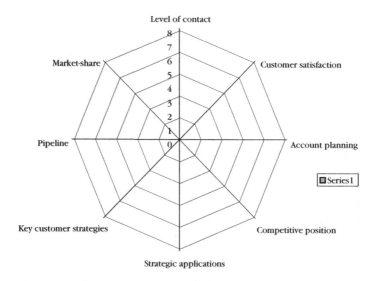

Fig. 10.1 An example of a spider's web.

account management is whether over a long period of time we win against the competition. Taking these critical success factors we can now get a pictorial image by drawing the spider's web. An example is given in Fig. 10.1.

9. SETTING THE ACCOUNT MANAGEMENT GOALS FOR THE ACCOUNT

First of all, here is a bit of revision on the attributes of a well-worded objective or goal. It must be:

- » **S**tretching
- » **M**easurable
- » **A**chievable
- » **R**elated to the customer
- » **T**ime-targeted.

In addition to account management goals, we must not forget that the team also needs to identify the key sales campaigns it intends to fight in the next relevant time period. In setting sales campaign goals there is a specific customer problem and a specific measurable solution for the team to propose. Account management goals are more difficult. They reflect the longer term relationship between the two companies and deal with the quality of that relationship as well as with other measures that are easier to quantify.

The SMART template is more difficult to apply to account management goals. The team will have to allow more flexibility without compromising the aim of a goal, which is to make it possible for the team to monitor its success in implementing the plan.

10. SETTING THE STRATEGY FOR ACHIEVING THE GOALS, AND CREATING ACTION PLANS

Some goals need little explanation. They are clear and it is easy for everyone to know what must be done. Others are by their nature more difficult, and it may be helpful to include a strategy statement between the goal and the activity plans. Once again keep it simple. The statement should help anyone who is involved in the goal to know how to behave. Here is an example of a strategy statement inside a market-share goal:

> "We shall achieve this market-share by emphasizing at all times our dominance in the overall market and our knowledge of hundreds of companies getting benefits out of our products and services."

It is useful to keep this in the front of the minds of anyone having something to do with the account. Everyone from a senior manager to a maintenance person will be encouraged to talk about other sites and companies that they have seen.

A customer satisfaction goal could have a strategy statement:

> "By making contact with all the key people on a daily basis, and answering letters within 24 hours."

If the team has completed a first-class SWOT analysis and followed it up with goals that meet all the criteria of the SMART acronym, deciding what to do is often straightforward. Once you know what you are going to try to do the detailed actions should flow reasonably easily.

The keys to good action plans are accountability and timescale. The team must allocate a willing owner to each and every action. The owners will then put a timescale on the action, taking into account other things they have to do.

A frequent problem at this stage is over-commitment. In the enthusiasm of the moment, when the team is starting to see solutions to problems which have been nagging away perhaps for years, team members will agree to do things additional to the tasks they already have in timescales which are not feasible. Make them take out their diaries and see if the short-term actions will fit into what is probably already a busy schedule. It is much better to lengthen the timescales and achieve them. If the timescales become so unsatisfactory that they threaten the goals or the mission, then the team is going to have to search for more resource.

It is useful to document the goals and action plans as a form (see Fig. 10.2). These forms altogether are actually the plan. The SWOT analysis is back-up material used to ensure that the plan meets the key issues of the account.

Goal				
Strategy statement				
Activity	Milestone	Time	Responsibility	

Fig. 10.2 Goal and action plan.

KEY LEARNING POINTS

The biggest single contributor to the production of a successful account plan is how well the team understands the main drivers of the plan – the customer's mission, objectives, and key issues. The least likely plan to succeed is one where the team starts from its own products and services and searches for opportunities for them anywhere in the customer's organization.

Frequently Asked Questions (FAQs)

Q1: How do you define account management?

A: Account management is a combination of selling solutions to customer problems to give this year's sales and profit streams, and putting in place and maintaining a strategy for working with the customer in a relationship that makes the next years of sales predictable and profitable. See Chapter 2.

Q2: Should a key account be a profit center?

A: If it is administratively possible, account managers should at least be aware of the gross margins they are producing and their own overheads. See Chapter 3.

Q3: What is a mission statement?

A: A short statement of the organization's aspiration. The best ones are practical and do not try to cover too many issues. See Chapter 10.

Q4: How long should a team spend on understanding the current situation before deciding on an action plan?

A: In general, the environmental analysis part of planning lasts three times as long as the action planning part. See Chapter 6.

Q5: How do I give all the stakeholders access to my account plan?

A: Use a consistent Internet or intranet template and give the stakeholders appropriate permissions to see the complete plan. See Chapter 5.

Q6: What is the most effective way of training account managers?

A: Use a blended solution of limited face-to-face training enhanced with on-line coaching and electronic tools. See Chapter 4.

Q7: Is there a quick way of measuring your performance in a key account apart from counting the sales?

A: Use a radar diagram measuring yourself against the key attributes of a well-run key account. See Chapter 7.

Q8: What is field training?

A: Simply training, or development, activity away from any formal setting, undertaken out and about on territory. See Chapter 8, Glossary of Terms.

Q9: Does a key account's annual report give an account team useful information?

A: Yes, in terms of the key account's strategy, key issues, and financial health. See Chapter 9.

Q10: In examining your weaknesses in an account, are bullet points sufficient?

A: No, you need a whole sentence to be able to see what you can do about removing the weakness. See Chapter 7.

EXPRESSEXEC –
BUSINESS THINKING AT YOUR FINGERTIPS

ExpressExec is a 12-module resource with 10 titles in each module. Combined they form a complete resource of current business practice. Each title enables the reader to quickly understand the key concepts and models driving management thinking today.

Available from:
www.expressexec.com

Customer Service Department
John Wiley & Sons Ltd
Southern Cross Trading Estate
1 Oldlands Way, Bognor Regis
West Sussex, PO22 9SA
Tel: +44(0)1243 843 294
Fax: +44(0)1243 843 303
Email: cs-books@wiley.co.uk

Index

Printed and bound by CPI Group (UK) Ltd, Croydon, CR0 4YY

13/04/2025

14656559-0005